At Issue

WITHDRAWN

What Is Humanity's Greatest Challenge?

Other Books in the At Issue Series:

At Issue

What Is Humanity's Greatest Challenge?

Roman Espejo, Book Editor

GREENHAVEN PRESS
A part of Gale, Cengage Learning

GALE
CENGAGE Learning™

Detroit • New York • San Francisco • New Haven, Conn • Waterville, Maine • London

Christine Nasso, *Publisher*
Elizabeth Des Chenes, *Managing Editor*

© 2010 Greenhaven Press, a part of Gale, Cengage Learning.

Gale and Greenhaven Press are registered trademarks used herein under license.

For more information, contact:
Greenhaven Press
27500 Drake Rd.
Farmington Hills, MI 48331-3535
Or you can visit our Internet site at gale.cengage.com

For product information and technology assistance, contact us at

Gale Customer Support, 1-800-877-4253
For permission to use material from this text or product, submit all requests online at
www.cengage.com/permissions

Further permissions questions can be e-mailed to permissionrequest@cengage.com

Articles in Greenhaven Press anthologies are often edited for length to meet page requirements. In addition, original titles of these works are changed to clearly present the main thesis and to explicitly indicate the author's opinion. Every effort is made to ensure that Greenhaven Press accurately reflects the original intent of the authors. Every effort has been made to trace the owners of copyrighted material.

Cover image © Images.com/Corbis.

LIBRARY OF CONGRESS CATALOGING-IN-PUBLICATION DATA

What is humanity's greatest challenge? / Roman Espejo, book editor.
    p. cm. -- (At issue)
    Includes bibliographical references and index.
    ISBN 978-0-7377-4314-2 (hbk.) -- ISBN 978-0-7377-4313-5 (pbk.)
    1. Social problems--Juvenile literature. 2. Humanity--Juvenile literature.
    I. Espejo, Roman, 1977-
    HN18.3.W465 2010
    306.09'045--dc22
                                                        2009039151

Printed in the United States of America
1 2 3 4 5 6 7 13 12 11 10 09

Contents

Introduction

On June 11, 2009, the World Health Organization (WHO) declared that the H1N1 virus, a novel strain of influenza, had entered the pandemic stage. The organization elevated its alert to Phase 6—the highest level of an infectious disease outbreak—because the virus had spread in the distinct zones of the United States and Australia, qualifying it as a global phenomenon. As of WHO's warning, 27,737 human infections of H1N1 flu and 141 deaths had been documented in seventy-four countries since emerging in Mexico three months earlier. This included more than thirteen thousand cases and twenty-seven fatalities in the United States.

Although evidence suggests that it is neither acquired from eating diseased pork nor had evolved exclusively from pigs, the virus has been called "swine flu" because the transmission of the H1N1 virus to humans has occurred, while sporadically, from direct exposure to ill pigs. A few years before, the H5N1 virus, or "bird flu," had become endemic in Asia. But the last influenza outbreak to become a pandemic occurred in 1961; it originated in Hong Kong and killed one million people worldwide. In fact, a mutant strain of the flu virus, known as the "Spanish flu," caused one of the deadliest pandemics in human history. Between 1918 and 1920, this virus sickened a staggering half-billion people—one-third of the earth's inhabitants at the time—resulting in tens of millions of deaths.

Strains of the flu virus are potentially dangerous to human health for several reasons. This highly contagious respiratory illness, unlike the common cold, can lead to serious complications such as dehydration, bronchitis, and a potentially lethal form of pneumonia, or infection of the lungs. For children, the nervous system and muscles of the heart and other parts of the body are especially vulnerable. The flu can also exacerbate existing chronic conditions in adults, such as asthma, congestive heart failure, and diabetes. Regarding H1N1 flu in particular, some experts maintain that it is relatively mild, but they fear that the virus could mutate into a more lethal strain, which happened during the Spanish flu pandemic. Some researchers also claim that people under sixty years of age may be less immune to H1N1.

Because of these factors, WHO contends that the H1N1 virus poses a threat on a global scale. On April 30, 2009, Margaret Chan, the organization's director-general, minced no words in an official announcement, declaring that "all of humanity is under threat."[1] In addition, she urged every nation to take action: "All countries should immediately now activate their pandemic preparedness plans. Countries should remain on high alert for unusual outbreaks of influenza-like illness and severe pneumonia."[2] Still, making enough doses of a vaccine for an entire population poses considerable challenges. For example, even in an era of modern medicine and technological advancement, providing immunizations against H1N1 for every American may take as long as until January 2010.

Some commentators, nonetheless, have come forward to critique statements and warnings about the H1N1 virus. Just before Chan's announcement, Vivienne Allan from WHO's patient-safety program refuted the purported claim that 152 people were killed by the disease in Mexico. "That figure is not . . . from the World Health Organization,"[3] she maintained, insisting that only 7 people had died. Others contend that the dangers of H1N1 flu have been exaggerated by the press, compared with normal occurrences of the illness. According to Belinda Ostrowsky of the Montefiore Medical Center in New York, "You never hear about the many people who die of regular seasonal flu because it doesn't get as much media attention."[4] For instance, in New York City, where an estimated two thousand residents die from seasonal flu each year, only eight deaths related to the H1N1 strain had been confirmed in the area in the days preceding WHO's declaration of a pandemic.

As the pandemic of the H1N1 virus progresses, the outbreak's chain of events, to some, points toward an emergency of catastrophic proportions. To naysayers, this is an implausible scenario creating a false sense of alarm and distracting from more pressing issues. In *At Issue: What Is Humanity's Greatest Challenge?*, the authors present their viewpoints on other crises facing civilization.

Notes

1. Quoted at www.who.int, April 29, 2009.
2. Quoted at www.who.int, April 29, 2009.
3. Quoted in *Sydney (Australia) Morning Herald*, "Only 7 Swine Flu Deaths, Not 152, Says WHO," April 29, 2009. www.smh.coml.au.
4. Quoted in Adam Lisberg, *New York Daily News*, June 7, 2009.

Overpopulation Is a Global Challenge

Morgan Winters

Morgan Winters is a writer based in Minnesota.

Unlike with the topics of energy and the environment, dialogue addressing the population crisis is lacking. Often misunderstood, overpopulation is viewed as a problem of developing countries and that there are too many humans consuming the planet's resources. However, it affects all nations, and even if consumption is reduced, a steadily growing population will eventually overwhelm the earth. The solution, therefore, will reduce consumption and stave off population growth while confronting family policy issues and negating opposition to population control measures. Action must be taken now, or else the choice to have a child will no longer be free.

Americans have a long history of inciting political action by shaking one problem under our politicians' noses to draw attention to another. It's like killing two birds with one stone. Liberals are notoriously less-than-fond of Big Oil's rabid profit margins, so we point out the obvious need for alternative energy. Then, because we don't want to come off as anti-business, we frame it as an environmental problem. But it is also an economic problem, a social problem, and a foreign policy problem. Our hope, however tenuous, is that the environmental issue is one that can bring everybody, liberal and conservative, together to address the oil conundrum. This has

Morgan Winters, "Peak Population," *Utne Reader*, August 12, 2008. Reproduced by permission.

proven to be a reasonably effective approach. While our energy crisis is far from solved, at least it is being talked about by both [2008] presidential candidates. Which is a lot more mic-time than they're giving our other global environmental catastrophe: the population crisis.

A recent report by the Population Institute notes that global population could increase from 6.7 billion to as much as 12 billion by 2050. Most of this increase is expected to occur in developing countries. In spite of these bleak findings, the closest thing to population reform coming from the right amounts to, "If the world's brown people would stop having so many babies, there'd be no crisis." In other words: Population is not our problem. On the left, sentiment has been that if we ease poverty and increase education in developing countries, the trajectory of global population will even itself out. Basically, solve two pressing problems and the third is a freebee.

Everybody's Problem

For the sake of argument, let's say that as global citizens, the growing number of people inhabiting the Earth is everybody's problem. It's also safe to say that, based on solid statistical evidence, there is a direct relationship between lower standards of living and larger family size. Yet there is no guarantee that addressing these quality-of-living issues will solve the population problem, in part because our definition of what constitutes a problem in population is fuzzy.

Population control—even of the most moderate variety, like simply advocating smaller families—is met with vehement opposition.

We are faced with a crisis not because there are too many of us for the planet to sustain, but because we are collectively using up more resources than the planet can produce. This isn't just true with valuable commodities, like oil and ore. The most basic of resources are growing scarce as well—food, potable water, wood. While reducing consumption in first-world countries will go a long way in addressing this problem, a population that just keeps growing will eventually overwhelm the planet, regardless of consumption. And as formerly impoverished nations achieve moderate prosperity, their consumption grows, likely negating any environmental benefits from reduced population growth via poverty aid. Therefore, a two-pronged solution is needed: reduced consumption and staved population growth.

It is widely believed that the U.S. population is in decline and has been for decades. Hence, the assumption is that limiting our own population won't address the global problem. This is untrue on two counts. First, as Utne.com noted in January [2008], the birth-to-death ratio in this country recently reached replacement level again. Second, a child born in a first-world country uses far more resources and therefore emits vastly more carbon than a child born in a developing country. Limiting births *and* limiting carbon emissions would be far more effective than addressing only one of these issues. This not only makes an impact within our own country, it sets an example for other nations as well.

Primary Obstacles

One of the primary obstacles to enacting effective international policies to curtail the population explosion is that, like climate change up until recently, there is no real consensus that the present global population is a problem. Many countries, including the United States, still actively encourage family growth through tax incentives and other pronatalist policies. Population control—even of the most moderate variety, like simply advocating smaller families—is met with vehement opposition. These objections are not based on science or even logic; they are informed by the human desire to live the way we wish, consequences be damned. Or, put more generously, the biological, mammalian urge to procreate without restriction. The only way to counteract this desire is to make it less profitable to have children.

Rather than giving tax credits to parents, we need policies that attend to educational inadequacies, create affordable food cooperatives, and ensure that all children have medical coverage. Tax credits are meant to provide funds for these necessary services to families. If food, healthcare, and education are provided, actively subsidizing procreation won't be necessary. This will increase the quality of life for families without punishing parents or promoting family growth.

Next, make birth control and voluntary procedures such as vasectomies and tubal ligations more widely available worldwide. For every unplanned pregnancy averted, one less little bundle of CO_2 [carbon dioxide] emissions is born. These changes are not anti-family. They are not a replication of China's one-child policy. They simply help with family planning and give equal standing to small families, large families, and single people by de-subsidizing procreation. Pair this type of response in Europe, North America, and wealthy nations around the world with poverty relief and education in developing countries, and we may begin to make a real environmental impact that our children, if we choose to have them, can enjoy.

Another barrier facing advocates of population control is that, historically, attempts to limit population growth have often been motivated by the wishes of dynastic Eurasian puppet masters to maintain their grip on the indigenous populations of desirable regions under their control. Put simply, this form of population manipulation is preemptive genocide. [Journalist] Nicholas Kristof offers an astute summation of the grimy history of population control in a review of a book on the subject in the *New York Times*. This damaging association between the tyrannical and the humanitarian motivations of limiting population bolsters the need for transparent and public worldwide policies. If these policies appear to limit African and Asian populations while France and the United States continue to reward large families, the campaign will be seen as ethnic manipulation rather than an attempt to solve a global emergency. And rightly so.

There is another telling lesson to be gleaned from the crusade to replace fossil fuels with alternative energy: the necessity of acting while we still can. It is beginning to seem that, if velocity continues to build, we may yet solve our energy conundrum. Of course, solving a problem and actually *fixing* it are two very different things. The one relies on scientific invention (something humanity is notoriously good at), while the other necessitates pragmatic action (something we find much more difficult). Things are still looking pretty bleak. But as the [President George W.] Bush stranglehold begins to weaken, it seems almost certain that we will continue the push toward alternative forms of energy.

Address the Problem Now

We may still dodge the bullet. Because of some long-overdue, forward-thinking policy adjustments—and more to come, one can hope—we may still be allowed a weaning period. In this scenario, energy costs will steadily rise. The poor will bear the brunt of the burden, as they always do in times of economic and industrial transition. But innovation will balloon, and the dividends of increased innovation will grow. If this is the case—and it is far from a forgone conclusion—it will be only because we made the right calls in the nick of time, in spite of heavy opposition from those unwilling to give up the luxuries they'd grown fat on. Any longer and we surely will be forced to forgo a transitional period in favor of more drastic measures.

And what of population? It is no stretch to assume that complacency and an unwillingness to make sacrifices, to self-regulate, will ultimately result in imposed regulation by government or nature. If we do not begin the process now—cautiously and with plenty of forethought, to be sure—our descendants, perhaps only a hundred years from now, will be faced with a crisis so dire that governments will be forced to drastic action.

It is baffling that, given the intense growing pains felt during the transition between fossil and alternative fuels, such concerns are scoffed at. A lack of fortitude and forethought in energy policy almost destroyed the planet, and still might. How much more difficult will it be, sometime in the near future, to make the argument that the choice to have a child is no longer a decision that can be made freely? Better to address the problem now, while we can still stomach the sacrifices a solution requires.

2

The Problem of Overpopulation Is Exaggerated

Philip P. Eapen

Philip P. Eapen is a Bible teacher and relief worker based in India.

Warnings against overpopulation are based on unsubstantiated claims, misconceptions, and doomsday predictions. For instance, the so-called population boom of the twentieth century is due to medical advances that have decreased infant mortality and prolonged human life expectancy, not spiraling birth rates in developing countries. Moreover, developed nations are among the most crowded, global food production is not in danger of being surpassed by consumption, and the planet's reserves of minerals, fossil fuels, and other raw materials are in ample supply. In reality, humans are living longer and better. Fears and concerns of overpopulation do not stand up to the facts.

W orld population reached six billion in the year 1999 and an estimated 83 million people are being added to that number every year since. Population growth was rather slow for most of human history. Famines, war, epidemics and high infant mortality rates ensured that population growth was negligible. Advancement in agriculture, food distribution and trade in the seventeenth century gave rise to a faster population growth in Europe.

The world population reached one billion by the beginning of nineteenth century. During the nineteenth century,

Philip P. Eapen, "Number Games: Exploding the Myth of Overpopulation," *Scribd (www.scribd.com)*, 2008. Reproduced by permission.

Europe's population doubled; Europeans spilled over to North America, South Africa, Australia, New Zealand, and other colonies they held in Latin America and Asia. The twentieth century began with a population of 1.7 billion after which world population saw a sudden increase, reaching two billion by 1930, three billion by 1960, four billion by 1974, five billion by 1986, and six billion by 1999. . . .

Taking population density into account, we get a more accurate picture of human population distribution in relation to total available land in every country or continent. This parameter will indicate that Asian and African countries are "people rich" while North America and Australia are "land rich." Very often, the perceived "population explosion" in Asian and African countries is about the high population density—or crowding—in these lands. Many European or developed regions are as crowded as some Asian countries while some Asian countries that have large populations have lower population densities. For example, the United Kingdom is more crowded than China; Germany is more densely populated than Pakistan!

There are several common reasons given in support of population control operations. These will be evaluated in the light of recent findings on the state of the world's resources, environment and on the real nature of "family planning" implemented in various developing countries. The following subsections explore common reasons that answer the question, "Why should we control population?"

Early Warnings

An early warning about uncontrolled global population growth came from Rev. Thomas Robert Malthus, the English political economist who wrote an "Essay on the Principle of Population" in 1798. The central thesis of this essay is that "population, when unchecked, increases in a geometrical ratio; and subsistence for man, in an arithmetical ratio." He argues that unless population growth is checked, humankind would soon face starvation. His views received wide acceptance especially among the upper classes of society because these "tended to relieve the rich and powerful of responsibility for the condition of the working classes, by showing that the latter had chiefly themselves to blame. . . ." A direct consequence of Malthusian views was a decreased interest shown by rulers for uplifting the poor. The rulers of the nineteenth century believed that "increased comfort would lead to an increase in numbers." Thus, poverty was considered to be a restraining mechanism that would curb the tendency of the poor to multiply.

The United Kingdom is more crowded than China; Germany is more densely populated than Pakistan!

Before Malthus, the Rev. Otto Diederich Lutken, in 1758, sought to dispel the idea that the prosperity of a state depended on its increasing population. He wrote,

> Since the circumference of the globe is given and does not expand with the increased number of its inhabitants, . . . since the earth's fertility cannot be extended beyond a given point, and since human nature will presumably remain unchanged, so that a given number will hereafter require the same quantity of the fruits of the earth for their support as now, and as their rations cannot be arbitrarily reduced, it follows that . . . they must needs starve one another out. . . .

The "Cancer" of Human Multiplication

[Professor] Paul Ehrlich's *Population Bomb* popularised Malthusian fears and predicted that the world would witness large scale starvation deaths in the 1970s. Ehrlich favoured coercive measures to control the "cancer" of human multiplication. Environmental agencies carry forward the Malthusian hypothesis with great zeal. An ardent supporter of Malthusian predictions once exclaimed, "If you are not hysterical, that just shows that you do not understand the problem."

The US Government organised an exhibition in the 1970s for school children in various parts of the country. It sought to spread this message:

> There are too many people in the world. We are running out of space. We are running out of energy. We are running out of food. And, although too few people seem to realize it, we are running out of time.

The Worldwatch *State of the World* report of 1998 expressed fears that the world is on the threshold of a large scale shortage of grain. It claims that the world grain productivity slowed down in the 1990s; a bleak picture of scarcity is portrayed in the report. [Worldwatch Institute founder Lester R.] Brown calls for major investments in agriculture as well as in population control.

Closely related to the worry about shortage of food is the worry about running short of resources such as forests, energy, mineral resources, and water. Rev. Lutken had mentioned this in his writing on the adverse effects of a growing population—the "other necessarily attendant inconveniences, to wit, a lack of the other comforts of life, wool, flax, timber, fuel, and so on." Therefore, he concludes that

> ... the wise Creator who commanded men in the beginning to be fruitful and multiply, did not intend, since He set limits to their habitation and sustenance, that multiplication should continue without limit.

How True Are Doomsday Predictions?

Over the past years there has been no dearth for doomsday predictions. The message that the world is going from bad to worse is so widespread and taken for granted in many quarters. The pertinent question is, how sure are we about our estimates of the carrying capacity of planet Earth? How true are these doomsday predictions?

Worldwatch Institute presents a gloomy picture of the world in its *State of the World* report:

> While economic indicators ... are consistently positive, the key environmental indicators are increasingly negative. Forests are shrinking, water tables are falling, soils are eroding, wetlands are disappearing, fisheries are collapsing, rangelands are deteriorating, rivers are running dry, temperatures are rising, coral reefs are dying, and plant and animal species are disappearing.

[Danish environmental scholar] Bjørn Lomborg, after careful research, points out that the doomsday predictions made by environmental agencies such as the Worldwatch Institute, Green Peace, and the World Wildlife Fund, and are then published by the popular media, lack integrity. Lomborg belongs to the school of [late economist] Julian Simon, who wrote extensively to expose various doomsday predictions related to human population growth. Contrary to the constant litany of doom, Simon's main argument is that things are getting better for mankind:

> My central proposition here is simply stated: Almost every trend that affects human welfare points in a positive direction, as long as we consider a reasonably long period of time and hence grasp the overall trend.

Lomborg agrees with Simon: ". . . by far the majority of indicators show that mankind's lot has *vastly improved.*" There are numerous indicators developed by the UN and the World Bank that can give us a fair idea about the state of a nation or the world. Before we look at any of these indicators, it is important to understand the nature of population "explosion" in the twentieth century.

An Achievement, Not a Problem

The sudden increase in world population in the twentieth century is primarily due to advances in medical care that brought down infant mortality and increased human life-expectancy. Contrary to what is popularly believed, "the increase is *not*, on the other hand, due to people in developing countries having more and more children." Lomborg cites UN consultant Peter Adamson's memorable words, "It's not that people suddenly started breeding like rabbits; it's just that they stopped dying like flies."

This, then, is not a problem but an achievement. Simon observes that while it took thousands of years for human life expectancy in the developed world to increase from twenty years to the high twenties, it took just two centuries for them to increase it to seventy-five years. Most of this increase took place in the twentieth century and Simon considers this as the "greatest human achievement in history."

In the developing world, in the beginning of [the] twentieth century, average life expectancy was below 30 years. Life expectancy has risen so rapidly in these countries that it is projected to cross the 70 year mark by 2020.

Too Many of *Them*

However, the good news of increased life-expectancy has become bad news for those who are interested only in the *relative* populations of Whites and Blacks, or, for that matter, the relative populations of the developed world and of the still-developing world. The issue then is not that there are too many people but that there are too many of *them*. This too is a pointer to a deeper spiritual disease that underlies modern anti-natalist claims.

An important human welfare parameter that contributed to the rise in life expectancy is infant mortality. In the developed world, the percentage of infants that did not survive fell from six percent in 1950 to less than one percent in 2000. Although developing countries have an infant mortality of six percent currently, it continues to fall and is expected to halve by 2020. Thus, the "scary" population explosion in the Majority World is a direct result of the advances these societies achieved in terms of primary health care.

This increase in the world's population represents our triumph over death.

Food Production Is in Step

Malthus and his supporters were wrong in assuming that food production would not keep in step with human multiplication. If resources were finite, and if there was no possibility for increasing a resource base, then the doomsday predictions of Malthus and his supporters would have come to pass. The resource base, however, kept increasing with increasing population. Babies came—with hands to work and minds to innovate—not just with mouths to consume resources. Ehrlich's warning that "the chances of successfully feeding and otherwise caring for an expanding population are being continuously diminished" does not stand up to facts. An FAO [United Nations Food and Agriculture Organization] study had this to report about global food production/consumption:

> How has agriculture responded to these increases in world population?... Production grew faster than population. Per caput production is today about 18 percent above that of 30 years ago. Food availabilities for the world as a whole are today equivalent to some 2700 kilocalories per person per day ... up from 2300 calories 30 years ago. And this is counting only food consumed directly by human beings. In addition, some 640 million tonnes of cereals are fed to animals for producing the livestock products which people consume.

Not only are we living longer; we are better fed now than was a smaller global population several decades ago. For instance, take the World Food Summit findings about the number of people who are starving today in the world. The percentage of starving people in 93 developing countries has decreased from 35% in 1970 to 18% in 1996, and will drop to 12% in 2010. Even though things *can* and *ought to* get better, the trend shows that things *are* getting better. This improvement has occurred in spite of the doubling of the world population during this period. Julian Simon is jubilant about this development:

> In the early nineteenth century the planet Earth could sustain only 1 billion people. Ten thousand years ago, only 4 million could keep themselves alive. Now, 5 billion people are living longer and more healthier than ever before. This increase in the world's population represents our triumph over death. I would expect lovers of humanity to jump with joy at this triumph of human mind and organization over the raw forces of nature. But many people lament that there are so many humans alive to enjoy the gift of life.

Simon's observation is on the mark. Among those who complain or worry about rising population, few complain about their own arrival on earth; neither do they think of making an early exit to lighten Earth's burden. Instead, they moan about the gift of life that God has bestowed on each new child!

Resources Are Not Running Short

The costs of minerals and other raw materials indicate that we are not running short of these resources. Although economists had shown beyond all doubt that we are not running out of fuel, minerals or food, environmentalists' claims to the contrary led Julian Simon to challenge such claims with a bet. Simon wanted his opponents to choose the resources of their choice and observe prices for a period of ten years. If any of the prices showed an increase, Simon was willing to pay $10,000. Although his opponents, all environmentalists from Stanford University, desired to win easy money, they lost the bet. All the resources that they had chosen—chromium, copper, nickel, tin and tungsten—and others that they left out such as petroleum, wool, cotton, minerals and food became cheaper. [*Christian Science Monitor* correspondent George] Moffett comments that the improved methods of detecting mineral reserves ensured that mineral reserves increased despite ever-increasing demand for these resources. He cites UN statistics to show how known copper reserves grew from 91 million tons in 1950 to 555 million tons in the early 1980s. So successful were Simon's arguments that, Moffett notes, the supporters of Malthus are now guarded in their use of the word "crisis" while referring to the effects of population growth!

Price of a commodity is an indicator of its scarcity or availability. The assumptions of doomsday predictors are proving to be false.

3

Global Hunger Must Be Addressed

Michele Learner

Michele Learner is a writer at Bread for the World Institute, a nonprofit humanitarian organization based in Washington, D.C.

Having doubled in the last few years, the prices of rice, wheat, and other staples challenge decades of progress against the world hunger crisis. These skyrocketing costs have taken a tremendous toll on the poor worldwide, with many falling deeper into poverty or suddenly unable to afford food. Factors contributing to the hunger crisis are higher fuel prices, environmental degradation and climate change, increasing demands for both grains and meat, and policies that prohibit exportation and distort the prices of crops. Short-term relief of hunger is necessary in the form of increased food aid and cash assistance; long-term agricultural reforms are needed to allow developing nations an equal chance to produce and sell their crops.

"I feel sad because I can't give my children the bread and vegetables they dream of."

—Raju Kumar,
33-year-old tea seller and father of three, New Delhi, India

The current hunger crisis, fueled by soaring prices for food, is taking an immense toll on the world's poorest people. In three years [2005 through 2007], global food prices have nearly doubled. The situation has worsened in the past few months [the first half of 2008], with dramatic spikes in the prices of rice, wheat, corn, and soybeans.

Michele Learner, "Responding to the Global Hunger Crisis," *Bread for the World Institute*, June 2008. Reproduced by permission.

For decades, the world has been making dramatic progress against hunger. The number of undernourished people has fallen from one person in every four in the 1970s to one in six today. Yet even before the current hunger crisis, the U.N. Food and Agriculture Organization estimated that 854 million people go to bed hungry. Today, the World Bank estimates that the rising food prices are putting an additional 100 million people at risk of falling deeper into poverty. This is a setback the world cannot afford to let happen.

Widespread Misery

"Of course I am happy when I eat. When I'm hungry, my stomach hurts, I don't feel like playing, I don't feel like doing anything."

—Jorge Luis Hernandez, 8 years old, El Salvador

In the morning, Jorge Luis eats a small bowl of rice and then goes to work picking coffee. Later, the World Food Program (WFP) helps brighten his day: While attending school in the afternoons, he receives a meal of rice, beans, and tortillas. It's his only full meal of the day.

Skyrocketing food prices are straining the budgets of families like Jorge Luis' and of the programs working to help them. WFP estimates that as a result of rising prices, an average family meal in rural El Salvador has 40 percent fewer calories than in May 2006.

It also reports that the cost of providing a meal for a schoolchild in Kenya has almost doubled recently, from nine U.S. cents to 16 cents. In April [2008], WFP warned that it would have to stop feeding 450,000 schoolchildren in Cambodia beginning in May unless it gets additional funding. "Rising prices have created a new group of hungry people," said WFP director Josette Sheeran, who "suddenly can no longer afford the food they see on the shelves."

Many hungry people live in countries that cannot produce enough food and must import it. Mauritania, where only a fraction of 1 percent of the land is arable, imports a large portion of its food. Recent price spikes mean that sometimes foods are not available for import at all. *The Washington Post* recently reported: "Food-producing countries from Argentina to Kazakhstan have begun to slam shut their doors to protect domestic access to the food they grow."

According to UNICEF, nearly half of all Indian children under three are undernourished.

Poor people in cities have been hard hit by the global hunger crisis. In the past year [2008] in New Delhi, where Raju Kumar lives, the price of lentils rose by 18 percent, rice by 20 percent, and cooking oil by 40 percent. According to UNICEF [United Nations Children's Fund], nearly half of all Indian children under three are undernourished. Kumar's children are among the many who long for bread and vegetables.

In rural areas, where three-fourths of the world's poor live, people are also suffering. Some can produce most of their own foods and have been relatively insulated from rising world prices. But most people do not own land or have enough acreage to grow sufficient food. Thus, most rural people must participate in the cash economy to meet at least some of their needs.

What about the United States? Most people have noticed the change in their grocery bills, particularly for some basic staples like eggs, milk, and bread. But for low-income Americans who were already struggling to make ends meet, higher food prices, higher energy prices, the subprime mortgage crisis, stagnant wages, and a higher unemployment rate combine for a bleak economic outlook.

Vicki Escarra, president of America's Second Harvest, reports, "We are seeing absolutely tragic increases nationwide in the number of men, women, and children in need of emergency food assistance, many for the first time ever." Food banks report that demand has risen by about 20 percent over last year [2007], while private food donations are down by about 9 percent, partly because of the weak economy.

Participation in the Food Stamp Program—which helps low-income families buy groceries—was up by 1.3 million people this January [2008] over the same time last year. By the end of 2008, the program is projected to serve nearly 29 million people every month.

The Food Stamp Program is a federal entitlement program: It must expand to allow everyone who meets the eligibility criteria to participate. But other nutrition programs for hungry and poor people—including school meals programs and the Special Supplemental Nutrition Program for Women, Infants, and Children (WIC)—operate according to budgets set in advance. The rising cost of food means that they must provide less help to participants or serve fewer people.

Why Is This Happening?

"We stand no chance against the hunger of richer countries."

—*Mame Kato Diop, fishmonger, Mauritania*

By the time a problem becomes a global crisis, many factors have contributed to it. It can be difficult to identify which causes are most important in a worldwide phenomenon, and some causes are specific to a region or food. That said, several factors stand out as driving the crisis of rising food prices.

The Energy Connection

Rising fuel prices are a key "supply" reason for higher food prices. When fuel sources cost more, it also costs more to bring farm machinery and supplies like fertilizer and seeds to the farm and later to get crops to market. It is more expensive to package and move food, whether from a farm community to a big city, a breadbasket region to a remote area, or an exporting country to an importer. All these costs are passed on to consumers.

That was true in the past as well, but there's a new wrinkle today. The development of biofuels means that food products can literally be fuel, and anything that can be made into fuel is in demand. Lester Brown, president of the Earth Policy Institute, explains: "The price of grain is now directly tied to the price of oil." As oil prices rise to new records, so do grain prices.

The Washington Post reported that [in 2008], about a quarter of the U.S. corn crop will be sent to ethanol plants rather than made into livestock feed, the use for which most U.S. corn has been grown. Iowa, one of the two biggest corn-exporting states in the country, has 28 ethanol plants. In the next couple of years, Iowa's exports of corn are expected to fall to less than half the current level. Nationally, stockpiles of corn are shrinking.

High prices for one commodity, like corn, affect a variety of other food sectors. For example, chickens eat feed made primarily of corn. Higher costs for people who raise chickens led to a 29 percent increase in the cost of eggs in 2007. The high price of corn is also an incentive for farmers to grow it. Two results: Fewer soybeans have been planted, and fewer acres have been left fallow in exchange for federal conservation payments. Owners can earn far more per acre by growing corn instead.

Environmental degradation and climate change are already having far-reaching effects on food production.

Developing sources of renewable energy is a primary goal of creating biofuels. In the long run, biofuels may also make energy more affordable. But decision makers must identify the best ways to get the benefits of biofuels while easing the unintended consequences for food crops, food prices, and hungry people.

The Weather Connection

Environmental degradation and climate change are already having far-reaching effects on food production, particularly in tropical regions of Africa, Latin America, and South Asia. In Africa's Sahel, warmer and drier conditions have led to a shorter growing season. Receding Himalayan glaciers in India mean more floods in the monsoon season and more water shortages in the dry season.

But we can't simply blame the weather—even extreme weather conditions like Australia's continuing drought. Australia is one of the world's top wheat exporters, and the drought has reduced its production by 98 percent in the past six years. However, more than 90 percent of the world's wheat crop is produced elsewhere.

Increasing Demand

Another key cause of increasing food prices is growing demand for food in the developing world. Hundreds of millions of poor people in China and India have escaped poverty in recent years. With higher incomes, they are, for the first time, enjoying more diverse diets. In addition to higher demand for food staples, there is rising demand for meat, which in turn increases the demand for grain to feed livestock.

The Wrong Policies

Clear-cut global supply and demand are not the only forces that determine prices for vital products like food. Countries make most decisions based on government or interest group priorities—not on what is good for global food security.

A prime example is government subsidies for farmers in the United States, Japan, and the European Union. Such policies often encourage overproduction and distort prices. They may even give farmers incentives that run entirely contrary to common sense.

For example, current commodity programs create an incentive for farmers to grow cotton in desert states like Arizona, where water for irrigation is scarce. In turn, artificially low prices for this subsidized cotton can prevent farmers in poor countries, such as Mali and Burkina Faso, from selling their cotton crops for a fair price and being able to feed their families.

Another national government policy that can come between supply and demand is the prohibition of certain exports. Some grain-producing countries have done this recently in an effort to keep domestic prices under control. Thus, less grain is available globally while demand has risen. The result is dramatic increases in the price of corn, soybeans, wheat, oats, rice, and others.

If market forces played a larger role, food prices would have risen more gradually and the world would have had more time to adjust.

In a recent series on the hunger crisis, *The Washington Post* reported that factors that interfere with supply and demand explain why "the global food trade never became the kind of well-honed machine" that has made the price of manufactured products increasingly similar worldwide. Some economists argue that if market forces played a larger role, food prices would have risen more gradually and the world would have had more time to adjust.

Industrialized countries also make policy decisions as to where to focus their development assistance. Devoting more attention and resources to improving agriculture is essential for a long-term solution to the global hunger crisis. Yet in the past two decades, total donor assistance for agriculture has been cut in half: from $8 billion in 1984 to $3.4 billion in 2004. Underinvestment in agricultural productivity is contributing to lower supply levels and thus to higher prices.

What Can Be Done?

> "We can only hope the world will listen, understand, and dig into their pockets to meet this extraordinary appeal."
>
> *—Josette Sheeran, Director, World Food Program*

In the short term, we must use every available means to provide more food and cash assistance for hungry and poor people. Some of these options are:

- increasing funding for international food aid for the World Food Program and other providers in the supplemental spending bill now moving through Congress;

- allowing the purchase of some food aid near its beneficiaries to reduce shipping time and costs;

- working with international organizations and groups in poor countries to coordinate aid;

- increasing benefit levels as well as participation in the Food Stamp Program;

- strengthening the Special Supplemental Nutrition Program for Women, Infants, and Children (WIC) and school meals programs;

- providing additional resources, indexed to inflation, for The Emergency Food Assistance Program (TEFAP) and other help for food banks; and,

- revisiting our energy policies related to biofuels.

Congress has opportunities to take these actions: in the supplemental funding request now being shaped, and in the FY2009 appropriations process.

In the longer term, key agriculture policy reforms in the United States, Europe, and Japan are needed to give farmers in developing countries a fair chance to produce and sell their crops. Reducing trade-distorting subsidies to U.S. agricultural interests is one critical step toward easing the current crisis in food prices and preventing the cycle from recurring. Unfortunately, Congress has missed this opportunity in the farm bill that it has just agreed to.

The hidden hope in this current global hunger crisis is the opportunity for hundreds of millions of poor people around the world who work in agriculture to benefit from the policy changes and increased attention to their situation that are being provoked by the surge in food prices. If ordinary citizens and their governments work together to respond to the current crisis, the dramatic progress against hunger that the world has seen over the last 30 years can resume with even greater urgency and resolve.

4

The Problem of Global Hunger Is Exaggerated

Gary Rethford

Gary Rethford is a contributor to the Philadelphia Trumpet, *the magazine of the Philadelphia Church of God.*

Famine rages in many parts of the globe, but popular notions of hunger are more deceptive than truthful. Food shortages do not exist: Hard-hit countries such as India—home to nearly half the world's hungry—are among the greatest exporters of food and agricultural products. Instead, the economic policies of wealthy and powerful nations disenfranchise poor nations, creating unfair markets, poverty, and starvation. Furthermore, armed conflict and corrupt governments, rather than weather conditions or a lack of food, have created famine in Africa and North Korea. The hunger crisis and prospect of global war are biblical prophecies of the return of Christ, which promises an abundance of peace and prosperity.

Today, famine rages over the Earth. Southern Africa is notoriously affected, but the world's attention has recently been focused on the Darfur region of Sudan, northeast Africa, where a United Nations World Food Program (WFP) survey of western Sudan residents revealed that "almost 22 percent of children under the age of 5 are malnourished and almost half of all families do not have enough food." The WFP fed more than 1.3 million people in the Darfur region in September last year [2004]. In addition, the same organization says the in-

Gary Rethford, "The Hunger Myth," *Trumpet*, March/April 2005. Reproduced by permission.

habitants of Haiti, Afghanistan, North Korea, Colombia, the Democratic Republic of the Congo, and Bangladesh are all suffering intensely from hunger.

From ThinkQuest come the following facts illustrating the world hunger problem: "In the Asian, African and Latin American countries, well over 500 million people are living in what the World Bank has called 'absolute poverty.' Every year 15 million children die of hunger.... The Indian subcontinent has nearly half the world's hungry people. Africa and the rest of Asia together have approximately 40 percent, and the remaining hungry people are found in Latin America and other parts of the world."

That hunger continues. Why? Simply because there is a lack of food? No!

Myths About Hunger

It is a popular notion that the main cause for world hunger is a lack of food. That thought contains a basket of truth, but a bushel of deception. Of course hunger and famine are the result of not getting enough volume or quality of food to support life, but that is not a foundational reason for the problem.

Even most "hungry countries" have enough food for all their people right now.

The myths about hunger are well documented in several sources. In his article "The Famine Myth," Dr. Leslie Jermyn of GlobalAware.org wrote, "Famine is a situation of chronic lack of food leading to eventual starvation and death for thousands or millions depending on the scale. It is not the result of singular causes like low rainfall or too many mouths to feed but results from *a long series of social, political and eco-*

nomic processes and policies." In that article, Dr. Jermyn lists three mythical causes for hunger: not enough food, too many people, and bad weather.

Peter Rosset, executive director of the Institute for Food and Development Policy, co-authored a book in 1998 titled *World Hunger: Twelve Myths.* "The true source of world hunger is not scarcity but policy; not inevitability but politics," said Rosset. "The real culprits are economies that fail to offer everyone opportunities, and societies that place economic efficiency over compassion."

An *Institute for Food and Development Policy Backgrounder*, based on the book, stated, "Abundance, not scarcity, best describes the world's food supply. Enough wheat, rice and other grains are produced to provide every human being with 3,500 calories a day. That doesn't even count many other commonly eaten foods—vegetables, beans, nuts, root crops, fruits, grass-fed meats, and fish. Enough food is available to provide at least 4.3 pounds of food per person a day worldwide: 2 1/2 pounds of grain, beans and nuts, about a pound of fruits and vegetables, and nearly another pound of meat, milk and eggs—enough to make most people fat! The problem is that many people are too poor to buy readily available food. Even most 'hungry countries' have enough food for all their people right now. Many are net exporters of food and other agricultural products."

To prove the point, India, which has been identified as home to almost half of the world's hungry, is Asia's second-greatest producer of wheat after China, according to the UN Food and Agricultural Organization (FAO). "This year's [2003] Indian wheat output, while revised downward, still shows a sharp increase over last year and the 2004 wheat area and output are estimated to be above last year and above the five-year average." India exports about 2 million metric tons of wheat per year.

The Politics of Food

"As the FAO states, 'There is no lack of knowledge about how to fight hunger'.... Economic policies, trade rules and corporate market power that sharply deepen the inequality between rich and poor are at the root of hunger."

Economic policies are one of the main causes of world hunger. Look at the wealthy and powerful of any nation whose people are starving. Are the elite starving? No—in fact, they are often grossly overweight. Why? *Because only the poor and disenfranchised of a nation starve.* That is the direct result of denying a nation's inhabitants the opportunity to own land for producing their food, or to seek gainful employment so they can purchase the food they need.

The "Green Revolution" was supposed to solve the problem of world hunger. It has failed because of the politics of food.

On occasion, even homeless people in America starve to death. That isn't because America doesn't have enough food; it has a superabundance. It's because, for one reason or another, some American citizens live on the streets of the richest nation on Earth and exist on handouts from others.

Increasing international food production, called the "Green Revolution," was supposed to solve the problem of world hunger. It has failed because of the politics of food.

"[T]he 'Green Revolution' sponsored by international support organs increased grain production significantly. Still, the book [*World Hunger: Twelve Myths*] notes that 'in several of the biggest Green Revolution successes—India, Mexico and the Philippines for example—grain production and in some cases exports, have climbed while hunger has persisted.'" *Poverty* is a main cause of hunger: Only those who have funds can afford to buy food; only those who own land can grow food. "As the rural poor are increasingly pushed from land, they are less and less able to meet the demand for food on the market."

International Trade Policies

Reducing world hunger by international trade agreements, such as the North American Free Trade Agreement and the Free Trade Area of the Americas, was based on the belief that greater trade in food would result in greater food security. The opposite is true. Feeding the world's hungry by promoting free trade has proven to be a colossal failure. As [the hunger-fighting organization] Oxfam Canada points out, exporting produce has caused greater insecurity because food has become a profitable commodity. Simply put, it's more profitable for a nation to sell at premium export prices than to sell at base price to the peasantry. In addition, the small farmer does not participate in these major trade agreements, so his interests and livelihood are not supported by them.

"For example, in 1999 wealthy OECD [Organization for Economic Cooperation and Development] countries spent $360 billion on agricultural subsidies, while total revenues for all developing nations from agricultural exports was only $170 billion. In other words, rich countries spent more than double the amount in subsidies that developing countries actually earned! Heavily subsidized agribusinesses produce more than is needed domestically. This cheap oversupply is then 'dumped' onto the markets of poor countries at prices less than the actual costs of production" (*www.oxfam.ca*).

"Dumping" undermines local economies because it artificially forces the market price down, and local farmers cannot compete. Therefore, because the developing nations lack international protections against these trade rules, economic policies, and the sheer power of major developed nations, they and their people fall victim to this practice.

The truth is, even in the category of trade, the world is divided into those who have and those who have not.

Wars and Rumors of Wars

The greatest fundamental cause of world hunger, far outstripping weather or any other single cause, is internal political and social unrest and conflict.

Of the major nations suffering famine, Haiti, Sudan, Afghanistan, Colombia and the Congo have been hit as the direct result of civil war and conflict that has driven populations from their homes and farms. In Zimbabwe, President Robert Mugabe urged that producing white farmers be forcibly evicted from their farms, promoting massive crop loss in the country. Civil war has been the single greatest contributor to world poverty and the death of its civilians. Sub-Saharan Africa is a prime example of this fact. In Sudan alone, it is estimated that 2 million inhabitants have been affected. The war in Afghanistan has dragged on for 22 years; civil war in Colombia has continued for 40 years. In the Congo at least 3.4 million people have been internally displaced by civil conflict.

In North Korea, the extreme shortage of food has been made worse by the government choosing to spend its money on feeding the army and military issues rather than obtaining food to feed its people. Andrew Natsios, former vice president of World Vision United States, wrote, "Former President Ronald Reagan stated our tradition best when he said: 'A hungry child knows no politics.' While every famine is complicated by politics, it is fair to say that the North Korean famine is the most complicated politically I have witnessed in more than 15 years. Politics is killing people. Literally."

Ethiopia is another nation that repeatedly suffers from famine. Today, it is once again on the verge of disaster, as reported by Stephanie Kriner of Disaster Relief. "As Ethiopia faces a possible repeat of the 1984-85 famine when at least 1 million people died, relief officials are scrambling for aid. At least 8 million Ethiopians are likely to face hunger or starvation this year, the United Nations said. And the warning signs that appeared in 1984 are showing up once again."

In her article, Kriner mentioned food shortages caused by drought over much of the last decade as the reason for shortage of food. In addition, distribution of food that has been donated by international relief organizations is impeded by "poor transportation and a lack of warehouses and distribution centers."

True, when analyzing causes of hunger and famine, weather conditions are a factor. But it tends to be a factor at the end of a long chain of events, not at the beginning. In the history of Ethiopia, the beginning cause of famine can be highlighted clearly.

Dr. Seyoum Hameso, author of several books, relates that in Ethiopia, the Great Famine of 1896 was the direct result of war conducted by Emperor Menelik, and became so intense that some form of cannibalism was practiced. The famine of 1973-74 was the result of Emperor Haile Selassie's war with Ogaden and Eritrea. In 1984, the famine was caused by the military regime of Mengistu Hailemariam, who conducted "war with Ogaden, war with Eritrea and Tigray, war with other oppressed nations, war within the establishment, and the red terror [of communism] against opposition groups. Mengistu's atrocities did not end there. . . . For millions of people whose voices are crushed and repressed, the place has been a hell for nearly a century."

Hameso lists wars continuing during the last decade between Ethiopia, and Somalia, Kenya and Eritrea. He includes the existing political corruption as a factor causing the loss of productive citizens, which has also continued the hunger problem. In addition, Ethiopia is one of the leading nations suffering from HIV/AIDS, further decimating the male population available for food production.

Famine and hunger are not primarily caused by a lack of food or disastrous weather. They are primarily caused by war and by corrupt, deceitful government. If we don't learn this lesson soon, it's going to get much worse!

5

The Oil Supply Crisis Could Be Humanity's Greatest Challenge

Matthew Simmons

Matthew Simmons is chairman and chief executive officer of Simmons & Company International, an investment bank.

The global economy has thrived on low energy prices and abundant supplies, and foreseeable shortages of oil and gas are its greatest threat. Over the past fifty years, reserves in the Middle East have been overestimated: Fewer than forty oil fields have been discovered in the last century despite intense exploration, key fields are almost depleted, and scant information on gas drilling is not encouraging. Moreover, as developing nations become industrialized, demands for energy are surging and bound to outpace supply. Thus, not only are peaks in oil and gas production on the horizon, cushions for accidents and disasters are too tight; one catastrophe could shut the world down.

For decades our conception of a serious global economic threat has been limited to wars or financial disasters. The possibility of energy issues morphing into economic disruptions faded as the world enjoyed decades of low energy prices and ample supplies. Over time, the energy worries that deeply concerned many public policy planners in 1973 and again in 1979 to 1981 became distant memories. The handful of serious energy students who warned of pending problems were usually dismissed by most energy economists and labeled as pessimists, contrarians, or alarmists crying wolf.

Matthew Simmons, "Shock to the System: The Impending Global Energy Supply Crisis," *Harvard International Review*, 28.3, Fall 2006. Reproduced by permission.

Unfortunately, the risk that the world might suddenly face a massive energy crisis never disappeared, even as oil and gas supplies grew from many new sources. Over the last three decades, the risk of a severe energy crisis crept inexorably closer as demand for oil and gas steadily grew while the supply of oil and gas matured. New discoveries of oil and gas over the last four decades were minute in comparison to early ones and were often from poor quality reservoirs. A growing percentage of world oil and gas supplies came from countries prone to political instability.

Since access to supplies of oil and gas underpins almost every aspect of modern society, there is perhaps no greater threat to the global economy than demand surging ahead of supply and triggering physical shortages. Only a massive war, pandemic, or global water shortage would inflict as severe a jolt to the world.

Miscalculation: How We Got Here

For the past 50 years, the world has blissfully assumed that oil and gas supplies were abundant and inexpensive to produce. Anchoring this cheap energy thesis were the beliefs that known Middle East oil reserves would last for 50 to 90 years and the comforting thought that most of the Middle East had barely been explored. Moreover, conventional wisdom assumed that producing Middle East oil was virtually costless. Thus, the only two major "risks" that worried energy observers were that a glut of cheap Middle East oil would wipe out supplies from safer regions or that geopolitical unrest would keep some supply from the market.

For some inexplicable reason, virtually no energy planner ever questioned this "Middle East Energy Abundance Theory," though little hard data, audited by third-party experts, ever existed to confirm it. For the past 50 years, the theory that Middle East oil was virtually inexhaustible was discussed so often in energy circles that it became codified into an "Energy Fact" needing no further proof.

What most energy observers missed was some basic information about the fragility of both Middle East oil and Middle East natural gas, documented in hundreds of technical papers. These were not necessarily easy to read and grasp quickly, but none were locked up in a secret vault.

Fewer than 40 giant and super giant oil fields have ever been discovered in almost 100 years of intense Middle East exploration for oil and gas. These comprise a significant portion of the world's roughly 120 giant oil fields. Of these, the 14 largest account for roughly 20 percent of all oil production.

The Golden Age of abundant and cheap Middle East oil is long gone.

These giant Middle East oil and gas fields were lined up like a convoy of tankers along both sides of the Persian Gulf. From the furthest northern field, Kirkuk, at the top of Iraq, there is a "golden energy triangle" extending about 1,100 miles to the eastern side of the Persian Gulf. The triangle's bottom leg extends 450 miles across the United Arab Emirates and the top of Oman. Its final leg goes back up to the triangle's top, just west of the Saudi Arabian side of the Gulf. Within this triangle reside virtually all the Middle East's giant oil and gas fields that have been supplying the world with inexpensive oil for 35 to 80 years.

The high quality light oil coming from some of the most productive reservoir rocks ever discovered is now rapidly being depleted. A high percentage of what were once key Middle East crude grades now come from shrunken sources. Current production targets in countries like Saudi Arabia and Kuwait are tapping pockets of oil left behind from the massive water injection program designed to sweep out all the "easy" oil these great fields could produce. Other new sources of oil supply are from thin oil "streaks" or oil being produced from very tight rocks or a combination of both.

The Golden Age of abundant and cheap Middle East oil is long gone. Middle East oil is now facing its Twilight Era. Saudi Arabia's great oil reserves are increasingly scarce: seven key fields produce 90 percent of Saudi oil, but the "sweet spots" of each of these fields are almost depleted. Abqaiq, the third-largest Saudi field, is now relying for its key extraction on previously bypassed "pockets" of oil. Current rates of decline approximate 8 percent each year, and spare production capacity has dropped from more than 5 million barrels per day in 2002 to less than 1 million this year [2006].

Middle East gas, also thought to be in vast supply, has barely been drilled, but the results to date indicate gas that is often sour and from very tight or ultra tight rocks. The sustainability and growth of Middle East natural gas is shrouded in secrecy, but the limited information in the public domain on key gas fields does not bode well.

A large percentage of the world's oil and gas supplies outside the Middle East also come from large fields now too old and new fields that are too small. The technology developed to find and extract oil merely allowed small fields to be exploited and oil and gas to be extracted at far faster rates. Technology did to a small extent enable the recovery of more oil and gas, but it did so mainly by "managing the tail end of a field's production"—allowing an almost depleted old oil field to continue to produce small volumes for an extended period. Clearly, this method has no long-term prospects.

Nonetheless, the world's energy consumers have blithely assumed their energy use could grow exponentially. No one warned them to curb their energy appetite. Forty years ago, when the world used only half the oil it uses now, global oil use was primarily confined to the USSR, Western Europe, the United States, and Japan. By 2006 every country embraces vehicles and lifestyles once only enjoyed in the world's wealthy countries. This change created an inexhaustible growth in oil demand. The various models forecasting oil demand by 2020 to 2030 all end up showing a world needing between 115 and 130 million barrels a day of oil use and demand for natural gas, 50 percent higher than today.

As astonishing as these demand forecasts sound, the estimates are based on relatively conservative assumptions: population growth will slow down, the global economy will become increasingly energy efficient, and developing countries like China and India will use far less oil and gas per capita by 2030 than a poor country like Mexico uses now.

Regardless of how conservative these forecasts for oil and gas demand might be, there is little chance that growth of any magnitude can occur. There is one energy rule that will never change: energy use cannot exceed available supply.

"See-no-evil" projections not only disguise the impending oil supply crisis, but they may contribute to its potentially catastrophic effects by keeping policymakers in the dark.

Given the rapid growth in demand for gas and oil, and the way many developing countries are rapidly mimicking South Korea or Singapore's economic growth over the past 20 years, the risk is high that energy demand for oil and gas will soon surge ahead of available supply. This will lead to energy shortages. Shortages encourage energy consumers to hoard, which in turn sends demand surging even higher.

Those who argue that this scenario is far too pessimistic depend upon a general hunch that new technology and high energy prices will soon yield vast new energy supplies. But this has been debated for almost a decade and so far, no groundbreaking technology has been developed to improve extraction and expand reserves. The last great oil frontiers were found almost four decades ago.

The Problem Today

Energy planners now need to grasp the high risk that the world's supply of both oil and gas is fast approaching its highest sustained peak supply. If this is true, stretching supply further now will naturally cause it to fall more drastically once the peak is reached. Unfortunately, rosy projections, like those of the US Energy Information Administration, suggest that oil production is unlikely to peak for several decades. Such optimistic forecasts often reflect the assumption that technological improvements will continuously enlarge reserves and allow more oil recovery. This assumption is belied by the production decline in fields throughout the world, such as Exxon's Prudhoe Bay, which continues to decline despite advanced recovery techniques.

Most important, the energy data on which these projections rely are often dated, highly speculative, and outright misleading. Demand estimates take years to verify. Of the world's proven reserves, 95 percent are "un-audited." There are virtually no field-by-field production reports, and supply data are imprecise and rarely objective. "See-no-evil" projections not only disguise the impending oil supply crisis, but they may contribute to its potentially catastrophic effects by keeping policymakers in the dark.

There is evidence to suggest that the peak is imminent, if it has not already arrived. Non-OPEC [Organization of Petroleum Exporting Countries] supplies are clearly nearing a peak, with five years of negligible one-to-two percent growth. Projections by the Association for the Study of Peak Oil and Gas, taking into account rising rates of decline in production growth and lower quality new oil, project the peak in 2008. But confronted with unreliable statistical projections, the best way to make an educated guess about peaking oil supply may simply be to observe where oil comes from. With increasing water incursion into reserves, serious problems with corrosion, and high risks associated with efforts to increase production, the world's most important oil production sites are simply in increasingly poor shape.

Demand outpacing supply is not the world's only energy dilemma. The safety and security of energy infrastructure raises a host of issues. The list of "flash points" where some dreadful event could suddenly affect energy supply grows every day. When terrorists attempted to attack Saudi Arabia's Abqaiq oil processing plant, it justifiably sent shivers up energy observers' spines. This massive complex, guarded by a series of chain-link fences, processes every barrel of light and extra light Saudi crude. Had the attack been successful, the world could suddenly have been without more than 6 million barrels per day of high quality oil for an extended period.

A final and more subtle energy risk receiving almost no attention is that most of our global energy infrastructure is silently rusting away.

The narrow and shallow Straits of Malacca are a conduit for almost 11 million barrels a day of Middle East Oil streaming to Singapore, China, Taiwan, Japan, and Korea. Terrorist attacks on only a handful of large crude oil tankers could shut off Asia's oil for what could also be a very long time.

Re-emergence of civil strife in Nigeria's oil-bearing Niger Delta, Venezuelan President Hugo Chavez's constant threats to cease selling Venezuelan oil to the United States, and threats by Ecuador and Peru to nationalize their oil resources—recently acted upon by the former country—all constitute risks to the steady flow of global oil.

Had the global oil and gas system maintained a significant cushion of spare productive capacity, the energy system could tolerate one or two of these unforeseen events. But that spare capacity was used up by steadily rising demand. Today, virtually all oil and gas fields produce at the highest rates they can sustain. The tanker fleet, the global drilling fleet, the world's high quality complex refineries are all at full capacity. Adding capacity to any of these will take years.

A final and more subtle energy risk receiving almost no attention is that most of our global energy infrastructure is silently rusting away. A high percentage of the world's key pipelines are well beyond their original design life. Many tankers and offshore drilling rigs are too old and were not maintained during the long period when oil prices were so low that few producers made any money. Experts now speculate that more than 25 percent of the world's offshore jack-up rigs are essentially technically obsolete. This summer [2006], we suddenly discovered that the United States' largest and one of its newer major oil fields, Prudhoe Bay, suffers serious corrosion problems, as do many North Sea oil platforms.

The world is now out of spare capacity of oil and gas at the wellhead. The world is also out of spare drilling rigs. Almost all of the world's key refineries operate at full capacity until their owners scramble to perform minimum refinery maintenance. The energy industry's workforce, from senior executives to blue collar oilfield workers, is graying. The oilfield depression lasted too long. Too many energy companies spent the last decade making sure they could survive a low-price environment and laid off too many skilled workers and hired no replacements. This lack of personnel will haunt the energy industry for the next decade or two. This deficit of human capital makes rig and refinery shortages even more complex.

How Bad Could Our Next Shock Be?

The oil and gas system is far too tight, with only tiny cushions to offset an accident, more corrosion problems, an earthquake, a hurricane or a terrorist attack on any of a long list of vulnerable sites. When the world last had two oil shortages, in 1973 and 1979, both were traumatic to the global economy. But they were easy to fix, as neither represented a permanent problem or a shortage lasting several years.

If a major accident happened to any of our petroleum highways, ranging from the Suez Canal or the Panama Canal to far more dangerous flash points like the Straits of Malacca, it would only take a matter of weeks before all usable crude and finished product inventories were used up and shortages began to shut down key parts of the global economy. If shortages trigger hoarding, the world's stores could soon be empty and its roads traffic-free. Only energy has the potential to shut down the entire world.

There is no way to completely prevent events that shut off key supply points. But the worse and more lasting problem would be for steadily growing oil demand to silently slide ahead of useable supply, creating a shortage with no easy fix. There is no way to deal with this issue other than the difficult process of reducing demand, but it may pose the gravest risk to the sustainability of today's global economy.

While many optimistic energy observers still argue that doomsayers or pessimists are wrong, the issue is now sufficiently serious that the optimists need to introduce more than tired phrases to the debate. If rosy projections turn out to be misguided—and over the past decade, none of the optimists' vocal arguments has borne out—the impending energy supply crisis could become one of the ugliest global tipping points that our economy has ever experienced.

6

The Oil Supply Crisis
Is Exaggerated

Tom Bethell

Tom Bethell is senior editor of the American Spectator *and a media fellow at the Hoover Institution.*

The theory known as Peak Oil that posits that oil production has reached a peak and reserves are now half-depleted and declining does not reflect reality. Estimates for global sources vary and are inclusive of future discoveries, and only one of up to 18 trillion barrels have been consumed. Rather, peak oil is an idea promoted by environmentalists who long for the age of alternative energy and the demise of fossil fuels and nuclear power. In fact, these activists hasten peak oil by stopping offshore and Alaskan drilling, and lawmakers, not shortages, cause oil "crises." Supporters of peak oil, however, are correct that prices will substantially increase, but this does not indicate that production has reached a plateau.

When I was in England [in 2008] my brother asked me if I knew anything about "peak oil." I wasn't too sure, to be honest. He is inclined to accept the theory, and even gave me a book to study, *The Last Oil Shock*, by a journalist called David Strahan. I read some of it and told my brother I would write an article about it. So here goes.

Peak Oil is the theory that the production of oil, worldwide, has reached a plateau and is now heading downward.

Tom Bethell, "Has Oil Peaked? Maybe Not," *American Spectator*, October 2008. Reproduced by permission.

Oil is the (supposedly) fossilized residue of animal and vegetable life and a "finite resource." So it's bound to run out sooner or later, as we are often reminded. (I wonder, though, if oil isn't abiotic [not from living sources], as [physicist] Thomas Gold thought. Maybe huge reservoirs exist at much greater depths?)

As [journalist] Peter Maass put it in a much-cited article in the *New York Times Magazine,* "peaking is a term used in oil geology to define the critical point at which reservoirs can no longer produce increasing amounts of oil." They say it happens when reservoirs are about half-empty. But that is a guess and one that seems to have been outdated by new technology. After this "peak" has been reached, Maass continued, "no matter how many wells are drilled in a country, production begins to decline." Then:

> The eventual and painful shift to different sources of energy—the start of the post-oil age—does not begin when the last drop of oil is sucked from under the Arabian desert. It begins when producers are unable to continue increasing their output to meet rising demand. Crunch time comes long before the last drop.

No one really knows how much oil is down there. The Saudis are secretive and oilmen who have made a big find have little incentive to tell you the details.

Estimates Vary

A key figure in the peak oil theory, almost its originator, was M. King Hubbert (1903–89), a Shell Oil geologist who predicted in 1956 that U.S. oil production would go into decline 15 years later. That turned out to be true. "Hubbert's Peak" occurred in 1970. He was elected to the National Academy of Sciences and became a professor at Stanford and Berkeley. He was also an advocate of nuclear power. Hubbert's method was then applied to worldwide oil production—a questionable extrapolation.

Anyway, Kenneth Deffeyes, Hubbert's former assistant and an emeritus geology professor at Princeton, then predicted that world production would peak at the end of 2005. His book *Beyond Oil* was published at about the same time. It is an article of faith among peakists that when you know the total producible quantity of oil worldwide, then the peak occurs "at the halfway point"; that is, when half of that oil has already been extracted. In 2005 Deffeyes said that total quantity was (close enough) two trillion barrels. Half of that had by then already been produced. Hence, the peak had just arrived.

Here's a different estimate by Nansen G. Saleri, CEO of Quantum Reservoir Impact and formerly the head of reservoir management for Saudi Aramco. In a March [2008] article for the *Wall Street Journal he wrote*:

> What are the global resources in place? Estimates vary. But approximately six to eight trillion barrels each for conventional and unconventional oil resources (shale oil, tar sands, extra heavy oil) represent probable figures—inclusive of future discoveries. As a matter of context, the globe has consumed only one out of a grand total of 12 to 16 trillion barrels underground. Big difference, and obviously there's a lot of uncertainty. No one really knows how much oil is down there. The Saudis are secretive and oilmen who have made a big find have little incentive to tell you the details.

An old friend, William Tucker, who is often reliable on energy issues, recently contrasted the optimistic view, summarized by [editor in chief of *Forbes*] Steve Forbes as the belief that the oil price is "a bubble" ([global financier] George Soros has said the same thing), with the pessimistic Hubbert's Peak idea. I met both Tucker and Forbes at a conference in upstate New York earlier this summer [2008]. Tucker had just written *Terrestrial Energy*, a book about nuclear power which I highly recommend.

But he also surprised me by siding with the pessimists on the oil issue. So much do I admire Tucker's work that he almost made a Hubbertian of me.

The Peakniks

I used the word pessimistic, but for the Peakniks the idea that oil production is on a downhill path is not gloomy at all. They long for it. If oil really has peaked, its price will rise so high that many of the social changes they have worked for all their lives will become realities. (I am assuming that they will also continue to block new nuclear power plants, as they have done for 35 years.) With peak oil a reality, and nuclear stymied, we will be destined to live in their solar-paneled, wind-powered utopia of bike paths and mass transit. The suburbs and SUVs will become obsolete, and air travel will be unaffordable for the lower orders. They want that to happen, but we in turn should be suspicious of predictions that are better thought of as hopes.

The leading advocate of peak oil today is Matthew Simmons, the president of Simmons & Co. International in Houston, specializing in the energy industry. He too wrote a book, *Twilight in the Desert: The Coming Saudi Oil Shock and the World Economy*. Described in the Maass article as a "card-carrying member of the global oil nomenclatura," Simmons predicted that the oil price, then $65 a barrel, would hit triple digits. And he "wasn't talking about low triple digits," he stressed. John Tierney, then a columnist for the *New York Times*, was one who read that prediction. He phoned Simmons and bet him that in 2010 the price of oil would not be as high as $200 per barrel (in 2005 dollars). Tierney knew little about oil production. He was simply taking the advice of a friend, the late [economist] Julian Simon, who had told him it was worth betting that the price of any natural resource would not go up over time. Famously, Julian Simon had bet Stanford's doom-saying ecologist Paul Ehrlich that the price of certain metals, worth $1,000 in 1980, would not have gone up 10 years later. Simon won the bet. By 1990 the value of the metals had declined by more than half.

In the new bet, Tierney and Simmons are each wagering $5,000, which will be put into a pot and paid to the winner on January 1, 2011. The oil price will be averaged over the whole of 2010 to minimize any sudden price swings. Julian Simon's widow shared the bet with Tierney.

Tierney must have been nervous this summer. Oil traded at its record high of $147 a barrel on July 11. Thereafter it swiftly dropped and as I write it is $33 below that peak. My guess is that Tierney will win, but political matters unconnected with oil reservoirs make things hazardous. Socialism, alas, is alive and well where oil is concerned. Nationalization is an ever-growing trend in the most promising oil regions, such as Russia, Algeria, Angola, Nigeria, and Venezuela. A Goldman Sachs analyst said that the alleged geological peak is really a geopolitical peak. Concern that war will erupt over Iran's nuclear ambitions is another worry. Mexico's oil production has steadily declined because the government treats its loss-making state oil monopoly Pemex primarily as an employment agency rather than an oil producer. That is the tendency of all state monopolies.

Today, there are no price controls, no shortages, and no crises.

Making "Peak Oil" a Reality

In the U.S., the Greens have done their best to make "peak oil" a reality, by stopping offshore and Alaskan drilling whenever possible. Fortunately, $4 at the pump has focused some minds. It's dawning on more and more people, even in Congress, that allowing the counter-productive drones called environmentalists to have so much influence over policy is a lunacy that must be curtailed. In my view, the great error of the peakists is their failure to understand the price mechanism. They see a rising oil price as an indicator that the "era of oil is over," or as reducing demand, as it has in the U.S. by 3.9 percent over the first six months of [2008] compared to last, but they fail to see it as eliciting more production. They don't think on the supply side. In fact, peak oil theory implicitly denies that price affects supply. (Nonetheless, U.S. crude production was 2.1 percent higher this July than last.)

Try Googling this: "Image: Oil Prices 1861–2007." What this dramatic chart shows is that the real price of oil fell almost continuously until about 2001, except for a period from the early 1970s to the mid-1980s. That bump up and down was brought about by the Arab oil embargo, which lasted for six months beginning in October 1973. Saudi production was cut by about 25 percent for long enough to demonstrate that no one else had the spare capacity to make up the difference. It was followed almost immediately by the U.S. folly of price controls. Price regulations on oil continued until President [Ronald] Reagan ended them on entering the Oval Office in January 1981. The effect of these controls was to discourage production at the moment when it was most needed, and true shortages ensued—periods when demand exceeded supply. By law, gas stations were not allowed to charge what motorists were happy to pay. Instead, they had to wait in line. The issue is not widely understood. One article I read online says that current oil prices are "well above those that caused the 1973 and 1979 energy crises." Wrong. Those "crises" were caused by U.S. lawmakers, not by world prices. Today, there are no price controls, no shortages, and no crises. As they always do, free market prices equalize supply and demand.

The key point is that the world oil price did not take off in an unmistakable way until a few years ago, and only recently have oilmen been confident enough to undertake expensive exploration without fearing they will be left high and dry if the oil price sinks back down again. The availability of that controversial thing called recoverable reserves depends on the price. Some years back there was a big oil find in North Dakota and Montana. It's called the Bakken Formation. [In 2008] the U.S. Geological Survey said that four billion barrels could be recovered. That was not what some had hoped, but it was 25 times larger than the estimate given for the Bakken field in 1995.

The Era of Cheap Oil Is Over

Developing oil at ever-greater depths takes time and capital and is at the mercy of the world oil price. Notice, by the way, that the 15-year period when Hubbard's peak came true was one of continuous, inflation-adjusted oil-price declines. Why should production increase when prices decrease? [In 2006] Exxon Mobil drilled almost five miles beneath the Gulf of Mexico, without hitting oil. Now, in view of the much higher price, another company is continuing to drill even deeper in the same location. Another number worth watching is the U.S. rotary rig count, provided by Baker Hughes, Inc., in Houston. The count peaked at 4530 in 1981 (when price controls were lifted) and had fallen to a low of 488 by 1999. By August 15 [2008] there were 1990 rigs at work.

The one concession I will make to the peakists is to agree that the "era of cheap oil" probably really is over. It does look as though we now face a permanent and perhaps substantial oil price increase. But that is not to say that production has peaked. Meanwhile, let's wait and see what the oil price is in 2010. Politics, national and international, will surely be decisive.

7

Global Warming Is Humanity's Greatest Challenge

James Hansen

James Hansen directs the NASA Goddard Institute for Space Studies, a part of the Goddard Space Flight Center in Greenbelt, Maryland.

The time bomb of global warming must be defused. Levels of atmospheric carbon dioxide produced by fossil fuels are pushing climate changes to tipping points that will spiral into disaster. The two degrees Fahrenheit warming seems innocuous, but is already stressing the ecosystem and has initiated sea ice melt, which could eventually lead to rises in sea levels that could wipe out shorelines, as well as exterminate countless plant and animal species and dry up freshwater supplies. However, reducing carbon dioxide emissions and moving beyond fossil fuels have been blocked by special interests. Immediately enacting a carbon tax, then, would reduce greenhouse gases, spur innovation in clean energy, and secure the planet's future.

My presentation today is exactly 20 years after my 23 June 1988 testimony to Congress, which alerted the public that global warming was underway. There are striking similarities between then and now, but one big difference.

Again a wide gap has developed between what is understood about global warming by the relevant scientific community and what is known by policymakers and the public. Now,

James Hansen, "Global Warming Twenty Years Later: Tipping Points Near," June 23, 2008. www.columbia.edu. Reproduced by permission.

as then, frank assessment of scientific data yields conclusions that are shocking to the body politic. Now, as then, I can assert that these conclusions have a certainty exceeding 99 percent.

The difference is that now we have used up all slack in the schedule for actions needed to defuse the global warming time bomb. The next President and Congress must define a course next year [2009] in which the United States exerts leadership commensurate with our responsibility for the present dangerous situation.

Otherwise it will become impractical to constrain atmospheric carbon dioxide, the greenhouse gas produced in burning fossil fuels, to a level that prevents the climate system from passing tipping points that lead to disastrous climate changes that spiral dynamically out of humanity's control.

Changes needed to preserve creation, the planet on which civilization developed, are clear. But the changes have been blocked by special interests, focused on short-term profits, who hold sway in Washington and other capitals.

I argue that a path yielding energy independence and a healthier environment is, barely, still possible. It requires a transformative change of direction in Washington in the next year.

On 23 June 1988 I testified to a hearing, chaired by Senator Tim Wirth of Colorado, that the Earth had entered a long-term warming trend and that human-made greenhouse gases almost surely were responsible. I noted that global warming enhanced both extremes of the water cycle, meaning stronger droughts and forest fires, on the one hand, but also heavier rains and floods.

My testimony two decades ago was greeted with skepticism. But while skepticism is the lifeblood of science, it can confuse the public. As scientists examine a topic from all perspectives, it may appear that nothing is known with confidence. But from such broad open-minded study of all data, valid conclusions can be drawn.

My conclusions in 1988 were built on a wide range of inputs from basic physics, planetary studies, observations of ongoing changes, and climate models. The evidence was strong enough that I could say it was time to "stop waffling". I was sure that time would bring the scientific community to a similar consensus, as it has.

If emissions follow a business-as-usual scenario, sea level rise of at least two meters is likely this century. Hundreds of millions of people would become refugees.

While international recognition of global warming was swift, actions have faltered. The U.S. refused to place limits on its emissions, and developing countries such as China and India rapidly increased their emissions.

Dangerous Tipping Points

What is at stake? Warming so far, about two degrees Fahrenheit over land areas, seems almost innocuous, being less than day-to-day weather fluctuations. But more warming is already "in-the-pipeline", delayed only by the great inertia of the world ocean. And climate is nearing dangerous tipping points. Elements of a "perfect storm", a global cataclysm, are assembled.

Climate can reach points such that amplifying feedbacks spur large rapid changes. Arctic sea ice is a current example. Global warming initiated sea ice melt, exposing darker ocean that absorbs more sunlight, melting more ice. As a result, without any additional greenhouse gases, the Arctic soon will be ice-free in the summer.

More ominous tipping points loom. West Antarctic and Greenland ice sheets are vulnerable to even small additional warming. These two-mile-thick behemoths respond slowly at first, but if disintegration gets well underway it will become unstoppable. Debate among scientists is only about how much sea level would rise by a given date. In my opinion, if emissions follow a business-as-usual scenario, sea level rise of at least two meters is likely this century. Hundreds of millions of people would become refugees. No stable shoreline would be reestablished in any time frame that humanity can conceive.

Animal and plant species are already stressed by climate change. Polar and alpine species will be pushed off the planet, if warming continues. Other species attempt to migrate, but as some are extinguished their interdependencies can cause ecosystem collapse. Mass extinctions, of more than half the species on the planet, have occurred several times when the Earth warmed as much as expected if greenhouse gases continue to increase. Biodiversity recovered, but it required hundreds of thousands of years.

The disturbing conclusion, documented in a paper I have written with several of the world's leading climate experts, is that the safe level of atmospheric carbon dioxide is no more than 350 ppm (parts per million) and it may be less. Carbon dioxide amount is already 385 ppm and rising about 2 ppm per year. Stunning corollary: the oft-stated goal to keep global warming less than two degrees Celsius (3.6 degrees Fahrenheit) is a recipe for global disaster, not salvation.

These conclusions are based on paleoclimate data showing how the Earth responded to past levels of greenhouse gases and on observations showing how the world is responding to today's carbon dioxide amount. The consequences of continued increase of greenhouse gases extend far beyond extermination of species and future sea level rise.

Arid subtropical climate zones are expanding poleward. Already an average expansion of about 250 miles has occurred, affecting the southern United States, the Mediterranean region, Australia and southern Africa. Forest fires and drying-up of lakes will increase further unless carbon dioxide growth is halted and reversed.

Mountain glaciers are the source of fresh water for hundreds of millions of people. These glaciers are receding worldwide, in the Himalayas, Andes and Rocky Mountains. They will disappear, leaving their rivers as trickles in late summer and fall, unless the growth of carbon dioxide is reversed.

Coral reefs, the rainforest of the ocean, are home for one-third of the species in the sea. Coral reefs are under stress for several reasons, including warming of the ocean, but especially because of ocean acidification, a direct effect of added carbon dioxide. Ocean life dependent on carbonate shells and skeletons is threatened by dissolution as the ocean becomes more acid.

Solution of the climate problem requires that we move to carbon-free energy promptly.

Such phenomena, including the instability of Arctic sea ice and the great ice sheets at today's carbon dioxide amount, show that we have already gone too far. We must draw down atmospheric carbon dioxide to preserve the planet we know. A level of no more than 350 ppm is still feasible, with the help of reforestation and improved agricultural practices, but just barely—time is running out.

A Move to Clean Energy

Requirements to halt carbon dioxide growth follow from the size of fossil carbon reservoirs. Coal towers over oil and gas. Phase out of coal use except where the carbon is captured and stored below ground is the primary requirement for solving global warming.

Oil is used in vehicles where it is impractical to capture the carbon. But oil is running out. To preserve our planet we must also ensure that the next mobile energy source is not obtained by squeezing oil from coal, tar shale or other fossil fuels.

Fossil fuel reservoirs are finite, which is the main reason that prices are rising. We must move beyond fossil fuels eventually. Solution of the climate problem requires that we move to carbon-free energy promptly.

Special interests have blocked transition to our renewable energy future. Instead of moving heavily into renewable energies, fossil companies choose to spread doubt about global warming, as tobacco companies discredited the smoking-cancer link. Methods are sophisticated, including funding to help shape school textbook discussions of global warming.

CEOs of fossil energy companies know what they are doing and are aware of long-term consequences of continued business as usual. In my opinion, these CEOs should be tried for high crimes against humanity and nature.

Conviction of ExxonMobil and Peabody Coal CEOs will be no consolation, if we pass on a runaway climate to our children. Humanity would be impoverished by ravages of continually shifting shorelines and intensification of regional climate extremes. Loss of countless species would leave a more desolate planet.

If politicians remain at loggerheads, citizens must lead. We must demand a moratorium on new coal-fired power plants. We must block fossil fuel interests who aim to squeeze every last drop of oil from public lands, off-shore, and wilderness areas. Those last drops are no solution. They yield continued exorbitant profits for a short-sighted self-serving industry, but no alleviation of our addiction or long-term energy source.

Moving from fossil fuels to clean energy is challenging, yet transformative in ways that will be welcomed. Cheap, subsidized fossil fuels engendered bad habits. We import food from halfway around the world, for example, even with healthier products available from nearby fields. Local produce would be competitive if not for fossil fuel subsidies and the fact that climate change damages and costs, due to fossil fuels, are also borne by the public.

A price on emissions that cause harm is essential. Yes, a carbon tax. Carbon tax with 100 percent dividend is needed to wean us off fossil fuel addiction. Tax and dividend allows the marketplace, not politicians, to make investment decisions.

Carbon tax on coal, oil and gas is simple, applied at the first point of sale or port of entry. The entire tax must be returned to the public, an equal amount to each adult, a half-share for children. This dividend can be deposited monthly in an individual's bank account.

Carbon tax with 100 percent dividend is non-regressive. On the contrary, you can bet that low and middle income people will find ways to limit their carbon tax and come out ahead. Profligate energy users will have to pay for their excesses.

Demand for low-carbon high-efficiency products will spur innovation, making our products more competitive on international markets. Carbon emissions will plummet as energy efficiency and renewable energies grow rapidly. Black soot, mercury and other fossil fuel emissions will decline. A brighter, cleaner future, with energy independence, is possible.

Time Is Short

Washington likes to spend our tax money line-by-line. Swarms of high-priced lobbyists in alligator shoes help Congress decide where to spend, and in turn the lobbyists' clients provide "campaign" money.

The public must send a message to Washington. Preserve our planet, creation, for our children and grandchildren, but do not use that as an excuse for more tax-and-spend. Let this be our motto: "One hundred percent dividend or fight!"

The next President must make a national low-loss electric grid an imperative. It will allow dispersed renewable energies to supplant fossil fuels for power generation. Technology exists for direct-current high-voltage buried transmission lines.

Trunk lines can be completed in less than a decade and expanded analogous to interstate highways.

Government must also change utility regulations so that profits do not depend on selling ever more energy, but instead increase with efficiency. Building code and vehicle efficiency requirements must be improved and put on a path toward carbon neutrality.

The fossil-industry maintains its strangle-hold on Washington via demagoguery, using China and other developing nations as scapegoats to rationalize inaction. In fact, we produced most of the excess carbon in the air today, and it is to our advantage as a nation to move smartly in developing ways to reduce emissions. As with the ozone problem, developing countries can be allowed limited extra time to reduce emissions. They will cooperate: they have much to lose from climate change and much to gain from clean air and reduced dependence on fossil fuels.

We must establish fair agreements with other countries. However, our own tax and dividend should start immediately. We have much to gain from it as a nation, and other countries will copy our success. If necessary, import duties on products from uncooperative countries can level the playing field, with the import tax added to the dividend pool.

Democracy works, but sometimes churns slowly. Time is short. The 2008 election is critical for the planet. If Americans turn out to pasture the most brontosaurian congressmen, if Washington adapts to address climate change, our children and grandchildren can still hold great expectations.

8

Global Warming Is a Myth

Ed Hiserodt

Ed Hiserodt is an aerospace engineer and author of Underexposed: What If Radiation Is Actually Good for You?

Scientific, meteorological, and historical records make a mockery of global warming. Record-low temperatures have recently been seen across the world; during the last decade, summers have become cooler and winters more harsh. Also, the earth has experienced cycles of heating that were far from cataclysmic as well as periods of cooling. Indeed, hundreds of scientists have come forward to dissent to the claim that the use of fossil fuels is creating climate change. And the go-to documents for alarmists, altered for political motives, assert that human influence cannot be clearly attributed to global warming. Ultimately, the movement to reduce carbon emissions would limit free markets and lead to corruption.

Judge: Counselor, do you have anything to say before I pronounce sentence on the accused?

Attorney: Yes, your honor. Might I remind you that the victim my client was accused of murdering showed up earlier and is very much alive, sitting there in the front row?

Judge: Sir, this court does not deal in trivialities.

Attorney: But your honor, I'd respectfully suggest that since there is no victim, there has been no crime and my client is obviously innocent.

Ed Hiserodt, "Whatever Happened to Global Warming?" *New American*, vol. 25, February 4, 2009, p. 10(8). Copyright © 2009 American Opinion Publishing Incorporated. Reproduced by permission.

Judge: Counselor, you are very close to being in contempt of this court. I am the one who determines guilt or innocence here and your client is going to hang.

Attorney: But judge . . .

In 1970, I recall New Orleans schoolchildren taking a 185-mile field trip to Jackson, Mississippi, so students might experience something they had never seen before: snow. This year [2009] they didn't have to bother, as Southern Louisiana was blanketed with four inches of the white stuff, the first major snow in 45 years, and only two inches shy of the all-time record of six inches set in 1895. It was also the earliest snow since record keeping began in 1850.

Not to be outdone, Las Vegas checked in with what local meteorologist Jerome Jacquest said was the most snow since 1979. With no snow removal or de-icing equipment, the airport was closed along with most roads. Gambling, however, was not affected.

Snow wasn't the only problem. Freezing temperatures in Denver set a new low of minus 18, eclipsing a record from 1901. White Sulfur Springs, Montana, reported 29 below, shredding the previous record mark of minus 17, set in 1922. For the week of December 15, 2008 alone, HAM Weather Service reports 1,537 record low temperatures in the United States and 1,110 record snowfalls—not exactly what one would expect while on the way to climate catastrophe owing to global warming.

Weather watchers know this isn't just an anomaly or freak occurrence. For the past 10 years, the summers have been cooler and the winters more severe. In Little Rock, for example, a chart in the newspaper shows there have been five consecutive months with average temperatures below normal. Since Little Rock is situated near the geographical center of the country, one would suspect that this is not an unusual condition, and indeed, such a suspicion is borne out by satellite measurements that cover the entire globe and are not subject to the "urban heat island" effect that has been shown to add as much as 10°F to recording stations in urban areas as compared to rural counterparts. An NBC crew sent out to show the Northwest Passage was ice free had their icebreaker stranded for three weeks because of thick ice.

With such obvious disputations of "global warming," one might also suspect that the convictions of some honest, objective members of the weather establishment would begin to waver—after seeing the victim alive and sitting in the courtroom.

Tip of the Iceberg

And in fact, it is apparent that more than just a few experts are wavering. When the news was reported of a British court announcing that [former vice president] Al Gore's *An Inconvenient Truth* was unfit for school "because it is politically biased and contains scientific inaccuracies and sentimental mush," CNN meteorologist Rob Marciano—who was off-camera preparing to give the weather report—applauded and said, "Finally, finally!" He was particularly incensed that Gore blamed Hurricane Katrina on anthropogenic (human-caused) global warming (AGW). During the period of December marked by low temperatures, mentioned above, CNN severe-weather expert Chad Meyer commented during *Lou Dobbs Tonight*, "You know, to think we could affect weather all that much is pretty arrogant."

In a July 18, 2008 widely circulated article entitled "No Smoking Hot Spot," Australian Greenhouse Office scientist David Evans came out of the global-warming skeptics' closet. Although having written the carbon accounting model used to measure Australia's compliance with the Kyoto Protocol [an international treaty designed to cut greenhouse gas emissions], Evans was wrestling with a problem: *the greenhouse-gas signature is missing.* If CO_2 [carbon dioxide] is the cause of global warming, then it must be absorbing solar energy and warming the air, which in turn warms the surface. Both alarmists and skeptics agree that all models predict a "hot spot" at 10 kilometers above the tropics. But there is no such hot spot. Quoting Evans:

> We have been measuring the atmosphere for decades using radiosondes—weather balloons with thermometers that radio back the temperature as the balloon ascends through the atmosphere. They show no hot spot. Whatsoever. If there is no hot spot, then an increased greenhouse effect is not the cause of global warming. So we know for sure that carbon emissions are not a significant cause of the global warming. If we had found the greenhouse signature, then I would be an alarmist again.

Global warming has become a new religion.

The Rest of the Iceberg

A U.S. Senate minority report entitled *More Than 650 International Scientists Dissent Over Man-Made Global Warming Claims*, subtitled *Scientists Continue to Debunk "Consensus" in 2008*, was released on December 11, 2008. These 650 dissenting scientists are more than 12 times the 52 government-supported scientists who gave us the 2007 Summary for Policy Makers—the abbreviated version of the climate assessment by the UN's Intergovernmental Panel on Climate Change (IPCC)—to which the major media looks adoringly for news about global warming. (There were, however, diplomats from 115 countries aiding the IPCC, making sure the warnings produced the greatest gloom and fear.)

The Senate report includes names, biographies, academic institutional affiliations, and quotes from hundreds of international scientists who have publicly dissented against man-made climate fears. Here are a few condensed remarks typical of the group as a whole:

- "I am a skeptic. . . . Global warming has become a new religion."—Nobel Prize winner for Physics, Ivar Giaever.

- "Since I am no longer affiliated with any organization nor receiving any funding, I can speak quite frankly. . . . As a scientist I remain skeptical. . . . The main basis of the claim that man's release of greenhouse gases is the cause of the warming is based almost entirely upon climate models. We all know the frailty of models concerning the air-surface system."—Atmospheric scientist Dr. Joanne Simpson, the first woman in the world to receive a Ph.D. in meteorology, and formerly of NASA, who has authored more than 190 studies and has been named "among the most preeminent scientists of the last 100 years."

- Warming fears are the "worst scientific scandal in . . . history. . . . When people come to know what the truth is, they will feel deceived by science and scientists."—UN IPCC Japanese scientist Dr. Kiminori Itoh, an award-winning Ph.D. environmental physical chemist. . . .

No study to date has positively attributed all or part (of climate change observed to date) to anthropogenic (manmade) causes.

International Panel on Climate Change

The IPCC, the entity that has generated the go-to documents that politicians and most media turn to for global-warming proclamations, doesn't have the credibility of the dissenters. The IPCC was formed in 1988 by the United Nations and the World Meteorological Organization. It is a single-purpose, single-interest organization. The entire reason for the IPCC's being is to provide evidence for anthropogenic global warming. Had it not been for the IPCC's activities, it is unlikely you would have ever heard the terms "global warming" or "climate change."

The IPCC has issued four "assessments" about the likelihood of AGW—in 1991, 1996, 2001, and 2007—and the likely effects around the world should catastrophic warming occur. These assessments are typically 800 pages or so in length and (except for the last one) without indices, making them virtually worthless for any but the most dedicated reader. But one might not bother reading them anyway, as the importance of the reports is completely eclipsed by the "Summary for Policy Makers" (SPM)—or as some would suggest, Summary *by* Policy Makers. This document is what is released to the media and, as we shall see, is often quite different from the report itself.

Let us look at how the IPCC "Summary for Policy Makers" handled the assessments written by committees of scientists. The following are statements from the original document of the second IPCC report, which had been approved by the scientific writers' committees. The first statement says: "None of the studies cited above has shown clear evidence that we can attribute the observed (climate) changes to the specific cause of increases in greenhouse gases."

That's pretty clear, so how about this one: "No study to date has positively attributed all or part (of climate change observed to date) to anthropogenic (manmade) causes."

There's not any waffling there, so let's look at one more: "Any claims of positive change of significant climate change are likely to remain controversial until uncertainties in the total nature variability of the climate system are reduced."

As Al Gore would say, that is "UN-EE-QUIV-o-cal."

Yet the three statements above were removed by the political influences, and in their place was substituted: "The balance of evidence suggests a discernible human influence on global climate." . . .

The IPCC and the Temperature Record

There is general agreement that the last ice age ended about 12,000 years ago. With the temperature some 20°F below today's norms and continuing that way for about 100,000 years, some 400 feet of the oceans' depth evaporated, fell as snow, was compressed into ice and covered the Northern United States to an estimated depth of one mile. With intermittent backslides and pauses, the Earth has generally been warming since that time. Yet the warming alarmists would have us believe that the warming that we have experienced recently is unprecedented, human-caused, and likely catastrophic. Oh really?

About 7,000 years ago, a warm period known as the Holocene Optimum coincided with the time that agriculture arose worldwide that, in turn, ushered in the Bronze Age. It is a period the IPCC simply ignores, as temperatures then were much warmer than their worst predictions under CO2-generated warming, yet catastrophe did not ensue. Polar bears had been around for the previous 190,000 years and survived the Holocene Optimum quite nicely, thank you very much.

After a few ups and downs, another warm period called the Roman Optimum is considered by historians to be a large factor in the rise of the Roman civilization, as society had the ability to produce more food than required to sustain the farmers, thus allowing others to construct the infrastructure of roads, buildings, and aqueducts upon which the empire was built. The Dark Ages, on the other hand, may not have been dark, but they were cold.

Then warmth came back in the form of what we call the Medieval Warm Period in about 950 A.D., known by historians as the Age of the Cathedrals. The Medieval Warm Period presents problems for alarmists because it can't be simply ignored. It is easy to prove that it was warmer than today. Not only do temperature proxies such as ice cores show it, but the flourishing Viking civilization on Greenland confirms it. Land that today is frozen solid then supported cattle, pigs, sheep, and goats for the "settlers." . . .

Sadly for our ancestors, the warm climate didn't last. Europe experienced a prolonged cold, wet spell, causing crop failures and famine. Always being on the verge of starvation resulted in a general weakness that is thought to have prolonged and exacerbated the "black death," which killed approximately half of Europe's population. This cool period—from which many climatologists consider the Earth to be still emerging—is known as the Little Ice Age. It too is a difficult period to explain away, as there are records of "frost fairs" on the Thames in London from the early 1600s to 1814, with ice on the order of 11 inches thick supporting tents, wagons, and even a visiting elephant. Since temperatures obviously have been increasing for several hundred years, is it so unusual for them to still be increasing? (Except that they're not.)

In North America the weather was cold enough for New York harbor to freeze so that one could walk from Manhattan to Staten Island. During the Civil War, army reports indicated that in Little Rock, for several weeks each year, wagon teams could cross the iced-over Arkansas River, something no one alive today has ever seen.

The period between about 1645 and 1715 was particularly cold and coincides with the Maunder Minimum, where only about 50 sunspots appeared, compared to an expectation of from 40,000 to 50,000. (More sunspots mean greater solar activity.)

Summing up, the Medieval Warm Period was far warmer than the temperatures global-warming alarmists expect us to reach, without any of the catastrophes predicted by alarmists, and the Little Ice Age clearly shows that Earth had a cold spell from which it has been warming for some 200 years, benefiting plant, animal, and human existence on Earth. Enter the "hockey stick."

The Hockey Stick

The term "hockey stick" refers to the shape of a 1998 graph of temperature versus time as displayed by global warmers Michael Mann, Raymond Bradley, and Malcom Hughes. It performs several amazing functions for the alarmists, namely:

- Eliminates the Medieval Warm Period;

- Eliminates the Little Ice Age; and

- Shows recent temperatures to be rising catastrophically.

It was a blessing for the IPCC and, according to Christopher Monckton—writer and producer of the informative and entertaining video *Apocalypse? NO!*—the hockey stick was used in full color no fewer than six times in the 2001 IPCC assessment report.

Unfortunately for Mann et al., two Canadians were suspicious of their results and finally were able to obtain sufficient information to challenge the methodology that produced the "convenient" graph. Businessman Steven McIntyre and economist Ross McKitrick examined the construction and use of the data set of proxies for past climate that Mann had used to estimate the temperature from 1400 to 1980 and found collation errors, unjustified truncation and extrapolation, use of obsolete data, and calculation mistakes. . . .

Good-Bye Free-Market Capitalism

If the IPCC and internationalists everywhere were content to let global warming remain an object of discussion and monitoring, its pronouncements would likely inspire the same type of humor as that elicited by an eccentric old uncle who tells about inventing the light bulb and sailing on the *Titanic*, but such is not the case. They want (demand) worldwide changes—decreasing levels of CO_2 emissions through a worldwide cap-and-trade system for CO_2. It is difficult to imagine any policy more destructive to our economy than "cap and trade." Today's bailouts are horrid and give government an equity stake in businesses—about as socialist as you can get. But "cap and trade" would gut the very system that has made the United States the wealthiest country in the world.

The possibilities for corruption are endless. It would make all U.S. enterprises beggars to controllers of the carbon-credit apparatus.

While there are a number of plans under discussion, most have the same basic elements:

- The government, or governments, would issue "carbon certificates" allowing a commercial or industrial user to consume a specified amount of carbon-based fuel. [Programs to extend this to individuals are already well underway in European Union countries.] The total amount would be *less than the currently used amount*, making these instruments instantly valuable. If, for example, a manufacturer desired to expand or continue production (since the number of existing credits would be continually reduced to meet some Kyoto-type protocol), he would be required to purchase them from another manufacturer or on "the open market."

- The "open market"—the reason Ken Lay [Enron's founder] and Enron were such fans of global-warming alarmism—could be anywhere in the world. A self-coronated potentate from Cowabunga, Africa, might sell the credits he is given by an international body for *not* destroying a rain forest (formerly known as a jungle) to an American entrepreneur who wanted to open a shoe-string repair business. Or an up-and-coming corporate executive might see a huge profit from moving his manufacturing plant to a Third World country (with no carbon certificate requirements), benefiting nicely from sales of the carbon credits obtained by closing his U.S.-based manufacturing plant.

The possibilities for corruption are endless. It would make all U.S. enterprises beggars to controllers of the carbon-credit apparatus. Carbon producers would become de jure criminals, and de facto criminals would become rich and powerful. Competition for the ever-decreasing credits would increase their value and the power the issuers had over our entire energy-dependent economy.

Fighting Alarmists

Saving the day may be a new organization, the NIPCC—the NON-Governmental International Panel on Climate Change. It has hundreds of scientists with varying backgrounds to show its objectivity. With bulldog Dr. S. Fred Singer at the helm, one should feel confident that the position of skeptics to climatic catastrophe will be well upheld.

Underpinning the global realism rebellion is the Petition Project of the Oregon Institute of Science and Medicine. Now with signed petitions from over 31,000 scientists with a minimum of a bachelor's degree, but including over 9,000 Ph.D.s, it is a force to be reckoned with now and in the future as the battle lines are drawn between skeptics and alarmists.

9

The Threat of Nuclear Proliferation Must Be Addressed

George P. Shultz, William J. Perry, Henry A. Kissinger, and Sam Nunn

George P. Shultz, a distinguished fellow at the Hoover Institution, was the U.S. secretary of state from 1982 to 1989. William J. Perry was U.S. secretary of defense from 1994 to 1997. Henry A. Kissinger was U.S. secretary of state from 1973 to 1977. Sam Nunn is a former U.S. senator who chaired the Senate Armed Services Committee.

While nuclear proliferation was necessary to maintain international security during the Cold War, a new and dangerous nuclear era is nearing. North Korea recently conducted a nuclear weapons test, and Iran refuses to halt its uranium enrichment program. More alarming is the increased likelihood of terrorists acquiring such capabilities. Nonproliferation measures are already under way, but urgent actions toward total elimination are essential. Steps to reduce nuclear forces in all nations, provide the highest standards of security for all stockpiles, and phase out highly enriched uranium can help achieve a future without nuclear weapons.

Nuclear weapons today present tremendous dangers, but also an historic opportunity. U.S. leadership will be required to take the world to the next stage—to a solid consen-

George P. Shultz, William J. Perry, Henry A. Kissinger, and Sam Nunn, "A World Free of Nuclear Weapons," *Wall Street Journal*, January 4, 2007. Reprinted with permission of The Wall Street Journal.

sus for reversing reliance on nuclear weapons globally as a vital contribution to preventing their proliferation into potentially dangerous hands, and ultimately ending them as a threat to the world.

Nuclear weapons were essential to maintaining international security during the Cold War because they were a means of deterrence. The end of the Cold War made the doctrine of mutual Soviet-American deterrence obsolete. Deterrence continues to be a relevant consideration for many states with regard to threats from other states. But reliance on nuclear weapons for this purpose is becoming increasingly hazardous and decreasingly effective.

North Korea's recent nuclear test and Iran's refusal to stop its program to enrich uranium—potentially to weapons grade—highlight the fact that the world is now on the precipice of a new and dangerous nuclear era. Most alarmingly, the likelihood that non-state terrorists will get their hands on nuclear weaponry is increasing. In today's war waged on world order by terrorists, nuclear weapons are the ultimate means of mass devastation. And non-state terrorist groups with nuclear weapons are conceptually outside the bounds of a deterrent strategy and present difficult new security challenges.

Apart from the terrorist threat, unless urgent new actions are taken, the U.S. soon will be compelled to enter a new nuclear era that will be more precarious, psychologically disorienting, and economically even more costly than was Cold War deterrence. It is far from certain that we can successfully replicate the old Soviet-American "mutually assured destruction" with an increasing number of potential nuclear enemies world-wide without dramatically increasing the risk that nuclear weapons will be used. New nuclear states do not have the benefit of years of step-by-step safeguards put in effect during the Cold War to prevent nuclear accidents, misjudgments or unauthorized launches. The United States and the Soviet Union learned from mistakes that were less than fatal.

Both countries were diligent to ensure that no nuclear weapon was used during the Cold War by design or by accident. Will new nuclear nations and the world be as fortunate in the next 50 years as we were during the Cold War?

Rekindling the Vision

Leaders addressed this issue in earlier times. In his "Atoms for Peace" address to the United Nations in 1953, Dwight D. Eisenhower pledged America's "determination to help solve the fearful atomic dilemma—to devote its entire heart and mind to find the way by which the miraculous inventiveness of man shall not be dedicated to his death, but consecrated to his life." John F. Kennedy, seeking to break the logjam on nuclear disarmament, said, "The world was not meant to be a prison in which man awaits his execution."

[Then Indian prime minister] Rajiv Gandhi, addressing the U.N. General Assembly on June 9, 1988, appealed, "Nuclear war will not mean the death of a hundred million people. Or even a thousand million. It will mean the extinction of four thousand million: the end of life as we know it on our planet earth. We come to the United Nations to seek your support. We seek your support to put a stop to this madness."

[U.S. president] Ronald Reagan called for the abolishment of "all nuclear weapons," which he considered to be "totally irrational, totally inhumane, good for nothing but killing, possibly destructive of life on earth and civilization." [Soviet leader] Mikhail Gorbachev shared this vision, which had also been expressed by previous American presidents.

Although Reagan and Mr. Gorbachev failed at [the 1986 summit in] Reykjavik [Iceland] to achieve the goal of an agreement to get rid of all nuclear weapons, they did succeed in turning the arms race on its head. They initiated steps leading to significant reductions in deployed long- and intermediate-range nuclear forces, including the elimination of an entire class of threatening missiles.

What will it take to rekindle the vision shared by Reagan and Mr. Gorbachev? Can a world-wide consensus be forged that defines a series of practical steps leading to major reductions in the nuclear danger? There is an urgent need to address the challenge posed by these two questions.

The Non-Proliferation Treaty (NPT) envisioned the end of all nuclear weapons. It provides (a) that states that did not possess nuclear weapons as of 1967 agree not to obtain them, and (b) that states that do possess them agree to divest themselves of these weapons over time. Every president of both parties since Richard Nixon has reaffirmed these treaty obligations, but non-nuclear weapon states have grown increasingly skeptical of the sincerity of the nuclear powers.

Strong non-proliferation efforts are under way. The Cooperative Threat Reduction program, the Global Threat Reduction Initiative, the Proliferation Security Initiative and the Additional Protocols are innovative approaches that provide powerful new tools for detecting activities that violate the NPT and endanger world security. They deserve full implementation. The negotiations on proliferation of nuclear weapons by North Korea and Iran, involving all the permanent members of the Security Council plus Germany and Japan, are crucially important. They must be energetically pursued.

But by themselves, none of these steps are adequate to the danger. Reagan and General Secretary Gorbachev aspired to accomplish more at their meeting in Reykjavik 20 years ago— the elimination of nuclear weapons altogether. Their vision shocked experts in the doctrine of nuclear deterrence, but galvanized the hopes of people around the world. The leaders of the two countries with the largest arsenals of nuclear weapons discussed the abolition of their most powerful weapons.

What Should Be Done?

What should be done? Can the promise of the NPT and the possibilities envisioned at Reykjavik be brought to fruition?

We believe that a major effort should be launched by the United States to produce a positive answer through concrete stages.

First and foremost is intensive work with leaders of the countries in possession of nuclear weapons to turn the goal of a world without nuclear weapons into a joint enterprise. Such a joint enterprise, by involving changes in the disposition of the states possessing nuclear weapons, would lend additional weight to efforts already under way to avoid the emergence of a nuclear-armed North Korea and Iran.

Reassertion of the vision of a world free of nuclear weapons . . . would be perceived as, a bold initiative consistent with America's moral heritage.

The program on which agreements should be sought would constitute a series of agreed and urgent steps that would lay the groundwork for a world free of the nuclear threat. Steps would include:

- Changing the Cold War posture of deployed nuclear weapons to increase warning time and thereby reduce the danger of an accidental or unauthorized use of a nuclear weapon.

- Continuing to reduce substantially the size of nuclear forces in all states that possess them.

- Eliminating short-range nuclear weapons designed to be forward-deployed.

- Initiating a bipartisan process with the Senate, including understandings to increase confidence and provide for periodic review, to achieve ratification of the Comprehensive Test Ban Treaty, taking advantage of recent technical advances, and working to secure ratification by other key states.

- Providing the highest possible standards of security for all stocks of weapons, weapons-usable plutonium, and highly enriched uranium everywhere in the world.

- Getting control of the uranium enrichment process, combined with the guarantee that uranium for nuclear power reactors could be obtained at a reasonable price, first from the Nuclear Suppliers Group and then from the International Atomic Energy Agency (IAEA) or other controlled international reserves. It will also be necessary to deal with proliferation issues presented by spent fuel from reactors producing electricity.

- Halting the production of fissile material for weapons globally; phasing out the use of highly enriched uranium in civil commerce and removing weapons-usable uranium from research facilities around the world and rendering the materials safe.

- Redoubling our efforts to resolve regional confrontations and conflicts that give rise to new nuclear powers.

Achieving the goal of a world free of nuclear weapons will also require effective measures to impede or counter any nuclear-related conduct that is potentially threatening to the security of any state or peoples.

Reassertion of the vision of a world free of nuclear weapons and practical measures toward achieving that goal would be, and would be perceived as, a bold initiative consistent with America's moral heritage. The effort could have a profoundly positive impact on the security of future generations. Without the bold vision, the actions will not be perceived as fair or urgent. Without the actions, the vision will not be perceived as realistic or possible.

We endorse setting the goal of a world free of nuclear weapons and working energetically on the actions required to achieve that goal, beginning with the measures outlined above.

10

The Threat of Nuclear Proliferation Is Exaggerated

William Langewiesche, interviewed by James Marcus

James Marcus is editor-at-large at the Columbia Journalism Review *and has been a senior editor and anchor for Netscape. William Langewiesche is the international correspondent for* Vanity Fair *and author of* The Atomic Bazaar: The Rise of the Nuclear Poor.

The pursuit of nuclear proliferation should not be demonized. Acquisition of such weapons is a logical step to achieve political power for a developing nation, which would not risk the consequences of such an attack. Pakistan's nuclear activities have created a greater degree of peace with neighboring India, for example. Hence, responses must be reworked to go beyond regulatory strategies, such as coordinating with tribal leaders, traffickers, and nongovernmental groups to intervene in the smuggling of enriched materials. The all-or-nothing paradigm of the Cold War has passed, and escalating attempts to halt proliferation, such as the Iraq war, have been destructive.

In his earlier books, William Langewiesche focused on large and fundamentally empty spaces: the Sahara desert and the sky (as transformed by the invention of flight). Recently, however, he has been drawn to more chaotic subjects. In *American Ground* he described the monumental ruin at Manhattan's Ground Zero, while *The Outlaw Sea* envisioned the ocean it-

James Marcus with William Langewiesche, "Going Nuclear: William Langewiesche on The Atomic Bazaar," *NewsQuake*, June 26, 2007. Reproduced by permission of the publisher and William Langewiesche.

self as a kind of watery Wild West. Now, in *The Atomic Bazaar: The Rise of the Nuclear Poor*, he takes on the burgeoning threat of nuclear proliferation. Netscape's James Marcus began a conversation with the author by asking him about the genesis of his new book.

William Langewiesche: The real basis for this book came from sitting in Baghdad, where I've spent a lot of time since 2003, and observing the catastrophe that has resulted from demonizing a political opponent.

Netscape: You're talking about Saddam Hussein.

Right. I was working for *The Atlantic* when I began this book. During the run-up to the 2003 invasion, we published a story with a cover illustration of Saddam Hussein—and it was an image of a demonic figure. I remember saying to my friends at the magazine, "We shouldn't be doing this. Let us not demonize this guy. It's a mistake."

And why was it a mistake?

If you believe that the very acquisition of a nuclear weapon by a Third World country is a sign of inherent evil, then you're in trouble. The fact is that nuclear weapons are extremely effective systems for achieving political power. And the decision to acquire them (though loaded with risk, of course, for the individual country) is actually a logical, rational move.

And what if Saddam Hussein had actually possessed nuclear weapons?

If you look at the specifics, at the tangible details on the ground, there's no evidence that Saddam Hussein would have been any more willing to *use* these weapons than we have been. Saddam Hussein was an extremely rational man. Sure, he was a bad guy, he killed lots of people. But it was all about consolidating his power. He was not going to use these weapons and see his country wiped out due to a nuclear response.

Deterrence was working, in other words.

Inevitable in the Third World

Right, and that's what led to *The Atomic Bazaar*. I kept thinking that nuclear proliferation is now inevitable in the Third World, and we can't be fighting a war like this one every ten years. I mean, let's look at Iran. Should we be willing to go to war to keep Iran from having nuclear weapons? The answer, quite clearly, is no. It's not a moral issue; it's a pragmatic one: we lack the capacity to win that war. So like it or not, countries are going to be acquiring these weapons, and it's best for us not to demonize them. Like it or not, we have limits to our power.

So the genie really has been let out of the bottle.

Proliferation cannot be stopped, all the more so since the Cold War is over. We're also much further away from the colonial mentality of subservience. So this issue is going to come up again and again and again. And we're going to have to figure out how to think about it, rather than becoming hysterical. The current attitudes toward nuclear proliferation are, at some extreme, a recipe for self-destruction.

Do we throw up our hands, then?

No, that doesn't mean we should accept it. That doesn't mean we should abandon diplomatic efforts to slow it down. But we have a whole range of options available to us, and we should understand exactly what we're fighting, and what it will cost us. This is not a dogmatic book.

The first two chapters seem to send a mixed message. They make the acquisition of a nuclear weapon by terrorists sound both alarmingly easy and reassuringly difficult.

Again, the mixed message is part of the reality. Our public conversation relies too heavily on argument instead of description.

And how does that factor into our conversation about proliferation?

Let's take the left wing. Their basic argument is, we abhor nuclear weapons, and therefore we believe that there should

be total, global disarmament: that will take care of the problem. It's a very formulaic, out-of-touch approach.

The right wing, of course, *loves* this stuff. They can manipulate it to boost the military budget, threaten civil liberties,
and all the other nefarious things they do in the name of
safety. Now, we need to acknowledge that the right is manipu-
lating the possibility of a nuclear terrorist strike in the most
despicable way. But that's not to say that there *isn't* an actual
possibility.

Living in a World Full of Risk

So what's the golden mean here, the middle path?

We should acknowledge the possibility but not manipulate
it. We should learn how to live in a world full of risk.

*Your description of the secret "nuclear city" of Ozersk in
Russia is absolutely fascinating. This couldn't have been the easi-
est piece of reporting, though, given the cloak of secrecy that sur-
rounds the place.*

I had to be a little careful. The FSB [Russia's federal security service] is all over the place, but I don't think they ever
figured out what I was doing. In any case, I'm used to that
kind of terrain by now. On the scale of anxiety, Pakistan was
way worse.

Way worse in terms of general paranoia?

That's right. But like I said, I've seen worse: I had major
problems in Sudan, and I just got arrested in the Congo a few
weeks ago. Accused of being a spy, the whole bit. In Russia, I
wasn't really worried. I like the Russians. The challenge there
was to talk around the subject, and not to be intimidated
away from it.

*Without knocking the efforts of various regulatory agencies,
you suggest that the ideal non-proliferation strategy will include
working with tribal leaders, drug traffickers, and other off-the-
grid types.*

If we want to interrupt the smuggling of fissile material, yes. I know it's very difficult politically for our government officials to do that. But we need to make contacts—lay trap lines, is the phrase I use in the book—throughout the wilds of the world. And that includes a number of key opium smuggling routes.

Doesn't that open the door to all sorts of ethical quandaries?

Oh, sure. You can just imagine some congressman from Utah getting morally outraged about this: "We are doing business with drug smugglers!" But I'm not talking about paying people off, or providing them with weapons. It's something much simpler: if these people have something of value, we should be the first in line to buy it.

We can do business, basically.

That's right, we can do business. We don't care if you're peddling opium. Now, there are parts of our government that *do* care, of course, and they're going to try and arrest you.

I see some potential friction there.

Look, most governments today tend to look at the world in purely governmental terms. Fifty years ago, when much of the world was purely governmental, that made sense. But now you see a world in which the nation-state means less and less, and is increasingly a formality. We have a very difficult time acknowledging that.

War on Disorder

Certainly your last two books have described a borderless and (in some sense) lawless world.

Oh, we don't have a difficult time acknowledging the lawlessness of the world—we're much concerned by it. What we're really conducting, in fact, is a global War on Disorder. But here's the confusing part: many of these disorderly places are not actually disorderly. They're just non-governmental. With the exception of a few weeks here and there, during periods of acute revolution and turmoil, there is some sort of organic power structure in place. It can be nominally criminal, or ideological, but it's always there. There's always something. And we do have the ability to tap into these power structures and work with them, even if we don't like them.

Do you see more of that happening down the road?

I see no sign that our current government is ever going to be capable of doing that. They're going to be increasingly disengaged in their world of formalism, and we will suffer the consequences.

Let's move on to the second part of the book. A.Q. Khan, who created Pakistan's nuclear program, is often depicted as a supreme villain—a kind of Pakistani Dr. Evil. But your portrait of him is much more nuanced. Describing his final period as a national icon and philanthropist, you write: "He had certainly lost perspective on himself. But the truth is that he was a good husband and father and friend, and he gave large gifts because in essence he was an openhearted and charitable man." Is he both—a ruthless weapons merchant and a decent guy? Not to mention a patriot?

By any definition, Khan was a patriot and an extremely effective agent for Pakistan's formal government policies. He was a damn good man to be running a nuclear weapons acquisition program. Was that evil? I would say that we shouldn't be thinking in those terms at all.

Is it a plus that Pakistan now has nuclear weapons?

It's obviously not desirable that countries acquire nuclear weapons. But if it's going happen, we need to look at these things with less outrage, less moralistically. And look, the argument is made in Pakistan (and it's not totally without foundation) that the acquisition of nuclear weapons has brought peace to the subcontinent. It does seem to have reduced the likelihood of conventional war between Pakistan and India. Both sides have calmed down a little bit. At least until the day when it all falls apart.

So Khan—who fell from grace and has been living under house arrest since 2005—is looking better and better.

If you look at Khan in professional terms, he did nothing wrong. He was an extremely good builder of nuclear weapons—and we have our own, of course. Is he deplorable on that level? No, I don't think so. On a personal level, it's indisputable that he went kind of crazy, in the same way that politicians or movie stars go crazy.

He got the celebrity disease, in short.

With that many people incessantly kissing my ass, I would go crazy too. I think it's an observable fact that by the end of eight years in office, our presidents have gone crazy as well. All of them! The best of them recover relatively quickly, and others don't. The current guy [George W. Bush] is nuts, and probably [Bill] Clinton was nuts too. I mean, how do you cope with it?

No doubt it's hard to keep your balance in that situation.

Khan didn't keep his balance. On a personal level, he was obnoxious as hell, with a highly inflamed ego. That confused him, and it's made what he's going through now much worse. He feels deeply, deeply betrayed by the political leadership of Pakistan.

We should resist nuclear proliferation, but acknowledge that, ultimately, we won't be able to stop it.

Disarming the Disarmed

Elsewhere in the book, you address the complaints of Third World proliferators like Khan, who question "the fairness of discriminatory nonproliferation tactics, and a world order in which the established nuclear powers keep trying to 'disarm the disarmed.'" Is the Nuclear Non-Proliferation Treaty [NPT] of 1968 discriminatory? Is it therefore useless?

The NPT is a highly discriminatory document. The question is: so what? That doesn't mean we should abandon the NPT, since it's the only effective diplomatic instrument we have. On the other hand, we also need to acknowledge that this discriminatory aspect of the nuclear world order is a major component in fueling proliferation around the globe.

Paradoxically enough.

That's right, and there's nothing we can do about it! In an ideal world, of course, we would all disarm. But that's never going to happen. People can march in the streets, feel good about themselves, then go home and have coffee—but it's not an effective way of looking at this problem. And since we're not going to disarm, we're stuck with a discriminatory world order in which the have-nots are resentful. That's the way it is.

Your ultimate message seems to be that nuclear proliferation is now a fact of life. What we need to do, then, is adjust to this new reality rather than attempt to stuff it back into the tube.

We should resist nuclear proliferation, but acknowledge that, ultimately, we won't be able to stop it. We also need to calculate what the various, escalating options will cost us. At one end of the spectrum is the NPT, which costs us very little aside from resentment, which would be there anyway. And at the other end, we have military intervention, which (as we've seen in Iraq) can be extremely self-destructive. In between there is a range of options, each of which has a price tag. We need to think calmly and rationally about these things, rather than apocalyptically. The Cold War paradigm of all or nothing is over. What we're looking at now is something in between.

11

The Problem of Global Poverty Is Improving

Howard LaFranchi

Howard LaFranchi is a staff writer for the Christian Science Monitor.

Progress has been made in the fight against global poverty, although the fight is by no means over. Since 1990, almost half a billion people have moved out of extreme poverty, and key indicators such as infant mortality and disease reduction are making significant progress. While this progress is encouraging, there are still many obstacles to overcome. International development aid fell in 2006 and 2007, and in 2005, more than five hundred thousand women died during pregnancy, which demonstrates how little progress has been made in improving maternal health. Some experts are also concerned that the progress that has been made has only reached the most accessible members of the population living in poverty.

Terrorism, climate change, and stretched food supplies may have grabbed more international headlines, but a more hopeful—even if less heralded—global trend is the considerable drop in the number of people living in extreme poverty.

Almost half a billion fewer people live in extreme poverty today than in 1990. And from Asia to Latin America and parts of Africa, key development indicators from infant mortality and primary education enrollment to disease reduction are registering considerable progress.

Howard LaFranchi, "Extreme Poverty the Focus at U.N. Summit," *The Christian Science Monitor*, September 24, 2008. Copyright © 2008 The Christian Science Publishing Society. All rights reserved. Reproduced by permission from Christian Science Monitor (www.csmonitor.com).

That's the good news that United Nations Secretary-General Ban Ki-moon will tout when he assembles world leaders ... for a midway review of the Millennium Development Goals for cutting extreme poverty in half by 2015. Since the world adopted the eight broad goals in 2000, some measure of progress has been made. And the UN's success in framing targets and rallying support from donor and recipient countries and the private sector for reaching them has boosted the international body's image and indispensability after years of seeing its relevance questioned.

Yet as Mr. Ban highlights the progress that has been made, he is also expected to draw attention to recent global trends that could make reaching any of the goals by 2015 more daunting:

- Skyrocketing food prices risk pushing millions of families that have risen out of poverty back down again;

- An ongoing global financial crisis could dry up aid from rich countries.

"A lot of encouraging progress has been made since these goals were adopted in 2000, particularly in a few specific areas like access to education, access to clean water, combating childhood diseases, and debt relief, and it's important to recognize the advances," says Robert Vos, director of the development policy and analysis division. "But significant gaps persist, even as we enter a period that may not be so favorable to additional progress unless we have renewed commitments all around."

Even before the most recent international financial turmoil, Mr. Ban was warning that development assistance from developed countries was falling—and he called on the wealthiest to recommit to past aid pledges. International development aid stopped rising in 2005, Mr. Vos notes, and fell in both 2006 and 2007.

Beyond that, summit participants will hear that the overall progress on the global development goals masks a widening divide between a fast-growing Asia and a lagging Africa. Progress is also uneven within developing countries, with some experts warning that the improvements registered so far have come largely in the most reachable and amenable sectors of the population.

What that's likely to mean, they add, is that the low-hanging fruit on the poverty reduction tree may have already been picked.

"The big challenge now is that, by and large, the parts of humanity still falling through the cracks, whether it's in Africa or Asia or Latin America, are the hardest to reach: the ethnic and linguistic minorities, the most remote of rural populations, the populations in conflict-affected countries," says Charles MacCormack, president of Save the Children and a longtime specialist in international development.

Little Progress Made on Maternal Health

Some development specialists worry that a focus on overall progress on the millennium goals will obscure a glaring failure to advance on a few key indicators, most notably on maternal health and reducing maternal mortality rates.

US officials say ... that the US is meeting all of its commitments, having more than doubled its foreign assistance since 2002.

"We are saying that [the goal of improving maternal health] is the goal where the least progress has been made ... and no one is disagreeing that that's the case," says Susannah Sirkin, deputy director for international policy at Physicians for Human Rights, an organization that advocates health as a human right.

Indeed, the 2008 report on the Millennium Development Goals declares that in 2005 more than 500,000 women died during pregnancy, and acknowledges that "little progress has been made in saving mothers' lives."

Noting that 99 percent of these fatalities occur in the developing world—and that almost all of them are preventable—Ms. Sirkin says the obvious conclusion is that they are the result of continuing discrimination against women. "We want maternal health to be recognized as an essential human right," she adds, "because rights imply obligations on the part of governments."

In calling the development-goals summit, Ban is following a model he initiated [in 2007] when he used the annual September opening of the UN General Assembly to hold a summit on global warming.

This year Ban says he is not looking so much for new commitments in development aid as for fulfillment of commitments already made. He also wants to remind the governments of developing countries, in particular in Africa, of the essential role that policy and efficient governance play in advancing development.

US officials say the American position going into the summit is that the US is meeting all of its commitments, having more than doubled its foreign assistance since 2002. They say that US foreign assistance is already focused on Africa, which is where the biggest challenges remain for even approaching the millennium goals by 2015.

Organizations to Contact

The editors have compiled the following list of organizations concerned with the issues debated in this book. The descriptions are derived from materials provided by the organizations. All have publications or information available for interested readers. The list was compiled on the date of publication of the present volume; the information provided here may change. Be aware that many organizations take several weeks or longer to respond to inquiries, so allow as much time as possible.

Action Against Hunger/Action contre la faim (ACF)
U.S. Office, 247 W. Thirty-seventh St., 10th Fl.
New York, NY   10018
Web site: www.actionagainsthunger.org

As part of the ACF International Network, Action Against Hunger is a relief organization dedicated to supplying emergency aid and providing long-term solutions to hunger, nutrition, sanitation, health care, and other humanitarian issues across the globe. ACF was established in France in 1979 and assists five million people in forty countries.

Bread for the World Institute
50 F St. NW, Ste. 500, Washington, DC   20001
(800) 82-BREAD (27323) • fax: (202) 639-9401
e-mail: bread@bread.org
Web site: www.bread.org

Bread for the World is a collective Christian voice urging the nation's decision makers to end hunger at home and abroad. By changing policies, programs, and conditions that allow hunger and poverty to persist, it provides help and opportunity far beyond the communities in which Americans live.

Cato Institute

1000 Massachusetts Ave. NW, Washington, DC   20001-5403
(202) 842-0200 • fax: (202) 842-3490
Web site: www.cato.org

Founded in 1977, the mission of the Cato Institute is to increase the understanding of public policies based on the principles of limited government, free markets, individual liberty, and peace. The institute aims to use the most effective means to originate, advocate, promote, and disseminate applicable policy proposals that create free, open, and civil societies in the United States and throughout the world. Its publications and reports embody libertarian stances on global warming, economics, and nuclear proliferation.

International Food Policy Research Institute (IFPRI)

2033 K St. NW, Washington, DC   20006
(202) 862-5600 • fax: (202) 467-4439
e-mail: ifpri@cgiar.org
Web site: www.ifpri.org

The International Food Policy Research Institute seeks sustainable solutions for ending hunger and poverty. IFPRI is one of fifteen centers supported by the Consultative Group on International Agricultural Research (CGIAR), an alliance of sixty-four governments, private foundations, and international and regional organizations.

ONE Campaign

1400 Eye St. NW, Ste. 600, Washington, DC   20005
(202) 495-2700
Web site: www.one.org

ONE is a campaign of over 2.4 million people from all fifty states and over one hundred of America's nonprofit, advocacy, and humanitarian organizations. Its objective is to raise public awareness about issues of global poverty, hunger, disease, and efforts to fight such problems in the world's poorest countries.

Stop Global Warming

15332 Antioch St., #168, Pacific Palisades, CA 90272
(310) 454-5726
Web site: www.stopglobalwarming.org

The Stop Global Warming Virtual March is a nonpartisan effort to bring citizens together to declare that global warming is here now and that it is time to demand solutions. It upholds that global warming is the most urgent issue of our time, and while the problem is of worldwide significance, it recognizes that the United States is the biggest emitter of greenhouse gases and doing the least about it. The necessary first step, Stop Global Warming states, must be to encourage Americans to take action.

United Nations (UN)

First Ave. at Forty-sixth St., New York, NY 10017
(212) 963-8687
Web site: www.un.org

Founded in 1945 to replace the League of Nations, the UN is an international organization that includes 192 member states, which are nations and territories of the world. Its aim is to protect human rights, enforce international laws, and promote social progress. Its agencies include the World Health Organization (WHO) and the United Nations Children's Fund (UNICEF). Among the UN's administrative bodies are the United Nations Security Council (UNSC) and Economic and Social Council (ECOSOC).

U.S. Department of Homeland Security (DHS)

Washington, DC 20528
(202) 282-8000
Web site: www.dhs.gov

The mission of the DHS is to prevent terrorist attacks within the United States, reduce America's vulnerability to terrorism, and minimize the damage and recovery from attacks that do occur. While the department was created to secure the country against those who seek to disrupt the American way of life, its charter also includes preparation for and response to all hazards and disasters.

World Health Organization (WHO)

Ave. Appia 20, Geneva 27   1211
   Switzerland
+41 22 791 21 11 • fax: +41 22 791 31 11
e-mail: info@who.int
Web site: www.who.int

WHO is the directing and coordinating authority for health within the United Nations system. It is responsible for providing leadership on global health matters, shaping the health research agenda, setting norms and standards, articulating evidence-based policy options, providing technical support to countries, and monitoring and assessing health trends.

Bibliography

Books

Michael C.
Carroll

Lab 257: The Disturbing Story of the Government's Secret Germ Laboratory. New York: Morrow, 2004.

Duncan Clarke

The Battle for Barrels: Peak Oil Myths and World Oil Futures. London: Profile Books, 2009.

Glynn Cochrane

Festival Elephants and the Myth of Global Poverty. Upper Saddle River, NJ: Allyn & Bacon, 2008.

Matthew
Connelly

Fatal Misconception: The Struggle to Control World Population. Cambridge, MA: Belknap Press of Harvard University Press, 2007.

Gorden Corera

Shopping for Bombs: Nuclear Proliferation, Global Insecurity, and the Rise and Fall of the A.Q. Khan Network. New York: Oxford University Press, 2006.

Al Gore

An Inconvenient Truth: The Planetary Emergency of Global Warming and What We Can Do About It. Emmaus, PA: Rodale Press, 2006.

William
Langewiesche

The Atomic Bazaar: Dispatches from the Underground World of Nuclear Trafficking. New York: Farrar, Straus & Giroux, 2007.

Bjørn Lomborg	*Cool It: The Skeptical Environmentalist's Guide to Global Warming.* New York: Vintage, 2007.
Aric McBay	*Peak Oil Survival: Preparation for Life After Gridcrash.* Guilford, CT: Lyons Press, 2006.
Jeffrey Sachs	*The End of Poverty: Economic Possibilities for Our Time.* New York: Penguin, 2005.
James Vernon	*Hunger: A Modern History.* Cambridge, MA: Belknap Press of Harvard University Press, 2007.
Alan Weisman	*The World Without Us.* New York: Picador, 2007.

Periodicals

Ronald Bailey	"Peak Oil Panic," *Reason*, May 2006.
Christie Brinkley	"Nuclear Proliferation: A Mother's Legacy," *Huffington Post*, May 13, 2009.
Christian Science Monitor	"How to Feed the Hungry Billion," January 29, 2009.
Boris Johnson	"Overpopulation Is the Real Issue," *Independent* (London), October 25, 2007.
Jason Kirby and Colin Campbell	"Life at $200 a Barrel," *Macleans*, May 28, 2008.

Jeffrey Kluger "Global Warming Heats Up," *Time*, March 26, 2006.

Michael Le Page "Climate Myths: Global Warming Stopped in 1998," *New Scientist*, August 15, 2008.

Mark Lynas "Food Crisis: How the Rich Starved the World," *New Statesman*, April 21, 2008.

Douglas A. McIntyre "The Cost of Swine Flu," *Newsweek*, April 27, 2009.

John Mueller "Radioactive Hype," *National Interest*, August 29, 2007.

Jay Nordlinger "How to Kill Poverty," *National Review*, June 30, 2008.

Robert J. Samuelson "Rx for Global Poverty," *Washington Post*, May 27, 2008.

Carl Zimmer "10 Genes, Furiously Evolving," *New York Times*, May 4, 2009.

Index

A

Abqaiq (Saudi Arabia) oil processing plant, 45, 48
Adamson, Peter, 21
Afghanistan, 35, 39
Africa, 30, 39
    hunger crisis, 35
    overpopulation problems, 14
    poverty in, 91, 93
Age of the Cathedrals, 72
AIDS/HIV, 40
Allan, Vivienne, 8
American Ground (Langewiesche), 83
America's Second Harvest, 27–28
Anthropogenic (human-caused) global warming (AGW), 68, 70–71
Arctic sea ice, 60–61
Argentina, 27
Asia
    hunger crisis, 35
    overpopulation problems, 14
    population growth, 17
    poverty in, 91, 93
    wheat production data, 36
The Atomic Bazaar: The Rise of the Nuclear Poor (Langewiesche), 84, 85
"Atoms for Peace" UN address (Eisenhower), 79
Australia
    Greenhouse Office, 68–69
    population growth, 17

B

Bakken Formation oil finds, 57
Ban Ki-moon, 92, 94
Bethell, Tom, 51–57
Beyond Oil (Deffeyes), 53
Big Oil industry, 10–11
Biodiversity, 61
Biofuels, 29–30
Birth control methods, 13
Bradley, Raymond, 74
Bread for the World Institute, 25
Brown, Lester R., 19
Bush, George W., 14, 89

C

Cambodia, 26
"Cancer" of human multiplication, 18
Carbon dioxide (CO_2) emissions, 13
Chan, Margaret, 8
Chavez, Hugo, 48
China
    increasing emissions, 60
    one-child policy, 13
    population density, 17, 18
    reduced oil/gas usage, 46
    wheat production data, 36
Christian Science Monitor, 24
Climate and global food crisis, 30
CNN newscast, 68
Cold War, 78–79, 90
Colombia, 35, 39
Comprehensive Test Ban Treaty, 81–82

D

E

F

G

New Zealand, population growth in, 17

Nineteenth century population data, 16–17

NIPCC (NON-Governmental International Panel on Climate Change), 76

"No Smoking Hot Spot" article (Evans), 68

Non-OPEC energy supplies, 47–48

North America
population growth, 17
poverty relief programs, 13
weather patterns, 73

North American Free Trade Agreement (NAFTA), 38

North Korea, 35, 39, 77–78, 80–81

Nuclear Non-Proliferation Treaty (NPT), 80–81, 89–90

Nuclear proliferation threat, 77–82
Comprehensive Test Ban Treaty, 81–82
as exaggeration, 83–90
need to address, 77–82
Non-Proliferation Treaty, 80–81, 89–90
nuclear power plants, 54
stance of U.S. leadership, 77–78
terrorist threats, 78–79

Nuclear Suppliers Group, 82

Nunn, Sam, 77–82

O

Obstacles related to overpopulation, 12–14

OECD (Organization for Economic Cooperation and Development), 38

Oil supply crisis, 42–50

as an exaggeration, 51–57
Bakken Formation oil finds, 57
China's reduced usage, 46
Europe's usage data, 45
fossil fuel limitations, 63
global usage data, 45–46
Green Revolution and, 55–56
inflation-adjusted prices, 57
Middle East oil, 43–47
movement to clean energy, 62
price regulations, 56
valuation of oil, 55

One-child policy (China), 13

Organization for Economic Cooperation and Development (OECD), 38

Organization of Petroleum Exporting Countries (OPEC), 47–48

Ostrowsky, Belinda, 8–9

The Outlaw Sea (Langewiesche), 83–84

Overpopulation challenges, 10–15
birth control methods, 13
birth-to-death ratio, 12
early warning signs, 17–18
exaggerations of problem, 16–24
fossil vs. alternative fuels, 15
as global problem, 11–12
possible solutions to, 14–15
primary obstacles, 12–14

Oxfam Canada, 38

P

Panama Canal, 50

Peak Oil theory, 51–57

Perry, William J., 77–82

Persian Gulf gas and oil fields, 44